Memories

of

Guildford

The publishers would like to thank the following companies for their support in the production of this book

Main Sponsor
LT Deeprose Limited

Biddles

DH Bryant Limited

Clarke Gammon

The Friary Shopping Centre

Lewis & Hickey

Mount Alvernia Hospital

Parsons Brinckerhoff

T&R Group

University of Surrey

First published in Great Britain by True North Books Limited
England HX5 9AE

ISBN 1 903204 22 4

Text, design and origination by True North Books Limited
Printed and bound in Great Britain

Memories

of

Guildford

Contents

Introduction

Memories? We all have them. Some are more accurate than most. Others have become blurred with time or fudged by remembering places and events as we would like to recall them, rather than how they really were. 'Memories of Guildford', will help you take a journey back in time. Indulge in flights of fancy or merely refresh your thoughts of how the town looked before shopping malls and fast food stores came along to dominate our lives. Younger readers can discover the past, and their parents and grandparents return to a time when cars managed to get out of first gear. In this book there is an opportunity to trace the changes that were made to the buildings and the lifestyle of Guildford people.

The photographs have been carefully chosen to represent a balance between people and architecture, between commerce and recreation. They are complemented by pithy and well written captions designed to tickle the memory cells into action and provoke discussion and disagreement about the quality of change that has come into all our lives as the 20th century unfolded. 'Memories of Guildford' is an opportunity to wallow in nostalgia for an age that has gone. Which parts of the past are worth reviving and which ones best forgotten is up to the individual. But, this book can help you highlight those issues or simply thrill in remembering those days of yesteryear. Sometimes we all need to just sit back and, to quote the 21st century waitress, 'Enjoy'.

This nostalgic look at the county town of Surrey would not be complete without being reminded of Guildford's place in British history over the last 1,500 years. The town was established at the east to west crossing of the River Wey in Saxon times. As it is situated on the north side of a gap by which the valley breaches the chalk ridge of the North Downs, it was well placed as a link for river and road. The Saxons are thought to have been here in the sixth century, but reference to the town first occurs in written records of the ninth century. Alfred the Great bequeathed his royal residence 'Gyldeforda' to his nephew. The town name developed from there, with 'gylde' possibly referring to the golden sand of the river bed and not to a medieval association of merchants or craftsmen.

Continued overleaf

From previous page

The town soon developed into an important centre and, before the end of the first millennium, was granted the privilege of minting its own silver coinage. Guildford developed around St Mary's and the present Quarry Street and was extended by housing that grew along what is now High Street. The names of some of the passageways leading off from them survive today as Tunsgate, Angel Gate and Swan Lane.

When William the Conqueror came to our shores the Normans built Guildford Castle, the county's only royal castle. The charter of 1257 raised the status of Guildford to that of county town. It flourished in the Middle Ages thanks to the thriving woollen trade and enjoyed enhanced importance in the 17th and 18th centuries as the Wey Navigation allowed barges to connect with London and coach travel opened up routes to

Portsmouth. Guildford was also the market town for large parts of Sussex as well as its own county. Satellite villages that fan out around the town still regard Guildford as their hub and use it as the shopping focus. Some might not regard this as a recommendation because traffic congestion has made getting into town an exercise in patience. However, once having got here, the rewards are tremendous. Guildford offers a rich mix of history to go with the variety of large stores and smaller specialist shops to which it is home.

'Memories of Guildford' is not meant to be a history book. It is a stroll back through more than a century of life that had a different agenda. It is a chance to leaf through pages that will remind you of sights, sounds and smells that have changed or are gone forever. This is your chance to rescue some of them from the out tray. Skate on the frozen floodwater of the Wey at the water

meadows near Shalford. Shop again at Harvey's for Dior New Look dresses or Mary Quant mini skirts. Take coffee on the roof garden and admire the fish in the ponds. Go up to the corner of Jenner Road and Epsom Road to watch a Kenneth More film at the old Odeon. For some alternative entertainment watch the schoolboys from Sandfield on the top deck of the bus. They piled to one side to make the bus sway as it took the corner. Then, cross over from there and buy a romper suit from Little People while dad pops into George Venn's to top up his tobacco jar with sweet smelling Arabian or Virginian mixture. Walk along High Street and sniff the roasting coffee beans as the scent wafts across the pavement near Abbot's Hospital. Head for Salsbury's for an attractive piece of jewellery and call in on your way for a glass of Whitbread Tankard costing two bob a pint at the Bull's Head. Then, record your thoughts using a pencil and notepad purchased earlier at Biddle's.

You are now nearly ready to turn the first page and bring back memories of the town that was the final resting place of Lewis Carroll. That fine 19th century novelist used his imagination to give us 'Alice's Adventures in Wonderland'. Now use yours to turn the looking glass on elegant buildings, jaunty shop awnings and people who talked of shillings and pence, quarts and gills, furlongs and yards. Put a stack of Film Fun comics and Famous Five books by your side to heighten the experience. Turn on the wireless for 'Workers' Playtime' or place on the gramophone a 78 record of Nat 'King' Cole singing 'Unforgettable'. With a glass of cream soda in one hand, a Kensitas cigarette dangling from the fingers of the other and a bag of misshapes from the sweetie shop on your knee, it is time to begin. Become an Ovaltiney once more or pin on that Robertson's golly badge. Get in the mood and let 'Memories of Guildford' bring it all flooding back.

Street scenes

The significance of the Guildhall and its magnificent clock is not just a matter of history. It also acts as a geographical point. Directions to a shop or place on High Street usually include such references as 'below' or 'above' the Guildhall clock. Its importance was recognised in the second world war when the clock was removed for safekeeping. It was stored, along with the town's treasures, in the cathedral crypt. This photograph dates from an age when the clock was safe from aerial bombing raids. The first flights by the Wright brothers were a decade away. This was the summer of 1893. Ladies strolled in pairs along High Street, protected from the sun by their dainty parasols that were as much a fashion item as a sun screen. They

seldom went out alone. Such behaviour was frowned upon. A chaperone, whether a relative or friend, was necessary in polite society. Next to the Borough Stores, the Guildhall flew the flag in honour of the forthcoming marriage of the Duke of York to Princess Mary of Teck. The wordy inscription below the balcony was typically prosaic and Victorian. 'Honour, riches, marriage - blessing long continuance and increasing hourly joys be still upon you.' The Victorians never used one word where fourteen would do! The wedding took place on 6 July. The couple eventually became King George V and Queen Mary. A year after she was widowed Queen Mary visited Guildford on 1 April 1937 to open a new maternity home in Stoughton Road.

Right: The piles of horse manure on High Street as the Victorian age came to an end were of more use than the car exhaust gases and engine oil spillages that blighted the environment in the 20th century. You can't put Duckham's on your roses and rhubarb, either. The road echoed to the clip-clop of pony and trap rather than the honking of horns by irate motorists. The authorities tried to limit the damage in later years when traffic access was restricted. At least shoppers can walk along the road again, though they are sometimes in danger from children whizzing along on scooters. Much of the character of the street as a special shopping experience has been retained. Although the proprietors and their wares might differ, the face of the buildings has largely been preserved. NatWest and LloydsTSB now occupy those just before the Guildhall. Sainsbury's and the Tudor Rose restaurant are across the road from there. In the 1960s women bought their shoes at Lilley and Skinner's before turning left through Tunsgate Arch. It was built in 1818 as the Cornmarket and Court Room, replacing The Tun, an old Tudor inn. The middle pair of its four pillars was spaced further out in 1935 to create a roadway into High Street. In the distance, far beyond the river, the Mount leads up towards the Hog's Back. Rising high on the skyline it is crossed by the A31 that runs out to Farnham.

Below: The procession celebrating Queen Victoria's Diamond Jubilee in 1897 has gone by. It is now time to take the tired children home. Wrapped in tender, loving arms or trundled along in a little boneshaker of a pram, these tots will sleep well tonight. As the mothers pass Waller Martin chemist's shop there is no need to call in for a draught to help their offspring nod off. They look to be well away without any assistance. Perhaps their dads have stopped off at the White Lion behind them. Situated on High Street, opposite the opening to Quarry Street, a noble lion overlooked the front door, keeping an eye on all those who crossed the threshold. The impressive building had its origins in a grand house built on the site by Richard Burchall in 1593. It was remodelled during the 19th century, evolving into the building seen here. Until the middle of that century it was an important coaching inn, particularly on the Portsmouth to London route. Its 60 bedrooms once did a good trade. The White Lion closed in 1956. When it was demolished in 1957 the initials RB, presumably referring to its original owner, were found in the chimney brickwork. Woolworth's then opened a branch on the site. That in turn was replaced when the White Lion Walk shopping centre was developed. A barrier now stretches across this part of High Street to restrict traffic access.

Bottom: As North Street celebrated the coronation of George V little knots of families and friends gathered to chat about this and that. They bought bags of hot chestnuts from street barrows, even though it was summertime. A barrel organ tinkled its melodies in the background. Street traders encouraged parents to buy a monkey on a ladder or a mechanical moneybox for the children. The scene was one of controlled excitement, a sort of polite fun. Women's long dresses swept along the cobbles and the feathered plumes in their hats bobbed in the breeze. They talked of the pageantry of the coronation celebrations. But, they would also have turned the conversation towards some of the changes that were coming to affect British society. Only five days before there had been a march through the streets of London by 50,000 supporters of the enfranchisement of women. The procession stretched for five miles. To make their point women dressed up as Boadicea, Joan of Arc and Queen Victoria as if to say that it was not just men who had an impact on important events. Factory girls mixed with aristocrats as they assembled in the Albert Hall. Just to underline the new order, Marie Curie won the Nobel prize for chemistry later in the year. As this day drew to a close a hubby might say to his wife, 'Let us go home, my dear. It will soon be time for you to prepare dinner.' She thought, 'Soon, very soon ....'

Right: North Street was gaily decorated in the summer of 1911. Flower chains, streamers and flags made the scene attractive for those enjoying a walk downhill towards the Methodist Church. It was an era of long coats and fine headwear. Even in the height of summer there was hardly an inch of adult flesh to be seen. Only the children had some part of their bodies exposed to the sunlight. Even that was kept to a minimum as little girls sheltered under large bonnets. The street was used as much by pedestrians as road users. The occasional motor car was still a novelty as horse and trap continued to be the more accustomed sight. The Methodist Church and its fine steeple came to North Street in 1894, replacing an earlier chapel built 50 years before. Methodism was the movement founded by John Wesley in the 18th century to revitalise the Church of England. The employment of lay preachers enabled the movement to expand rapidly throughout the 19th century. Methodism was more successful in the expanding industrial areas, where it helped the working people to overcome economic depression by spiritual means. It encouraged thrift and simple living as a means of raising economic status. The church was demolished in the early 1970s. This northern side of North Street has lost many of the proud buildings that once stood there. Newer ones, such as the Barclays building and Norwich House, cannot compete with the distinctive architecture that once graced North Street.

Above: The High Street, viewed from Market Street, showed just how patriotic we were in 1935. Union flags flew from lampposts and poles, or were draped from windows. Pretty triangles of coloured cloth blew jauntily in the breeze. We have had our moments on similar occasions since. When cynics say that patriotism is dead remind them of 1977. We held our street parties and had our bunting flying just as proudly when Queen Elizabeth II celebrated 25 years on the throne. Who can forget the joyous scenes in 1981 when her son, Prince Charles, married the beautiful Diana Spencer? Her place in our hearts was displayed in the public mourning that occurred when she lost her life in 1997. It seems to be the modern thing to knock royalty; yet, special events affecting the Royal Family have often been an occasion when the nation has come together. When Guildford rejoiced that George V had reached the 25th anniversary of his accession to the throne it was a chance to appreciate the good things in life. We could give thanks for the pleasure that Jack Hobbs had given us: Surrey and England's greatest batsman announced his retirement after a career that had brought him 197 first class centuries. There had been a thrilling FA Cup Final, won 4-2 by Sheffield Wednesday. It was the year that Malcolm Campbell smashed the 300 mph land speed barrier in Bluebird. Unemployment had fallen by over a million in the last three years.

Below: Looking up High Street we can see the flags and bunting flying in celebration of 25 years of the monarch's reign. George V succeeded his father, Edward VII, as King on 6 May 1910. He had served in the navy until 1892, hence his nickname 'the sailor king'. He is supposed to be the only British monarch to have sported a tattoo. King George was popular with his subjects for his down to earth manner. He was fiercely patriotic. He once said, 'I don't like abroad, I've been there.' Another famous comment, expressing his rude opinion of Bognor, is best not put into print here! The hotel on the left is the Angel. It is the last of Guildford's four coaching inns to survive. Built in the early 16th century, the Angel is a grade II listed building. Its timber frame, impressive internal panelling, grand fireplace and medieval vaulted bar remain as links to the days when it was a post house on the London to Portsmouth route. Then the coaches clattered their way through the archway into the courtyard and stabling area at the rear. This popular and lucrative trade disappeared almost overnight when the steam trains began puffing their way out of Guildford station. The Regency style facade no longer looked down on dusty passengers who came inside to slake their thirst. It is now more likely to welcome youngsters jabbering into mobile phones and trendies attempting to impress those close to them by accessing their stockbroker through WAP links to the internet.

Above: The portcullis had been put up at the bottom of High Street, as part of the 1935 celebrations, to balance with the rose arch near Holy Trinity. The motor cycle and sidecar passing over Town Bridge was a popular, if draughty, mode of transport. The only protection the rider wore was a flat hat to keep his head warm. Most motor cyclists had little time for crash helmets. Even those that were worn were little more than leather hats. The sidecar passenger was vulnerable in road accidents as the cab was quite flimsy. The area around the bridge is quite different today. The car approaching the camera can no longer go straight ahead. It now has the choice of turning to its left past Debenhams or to its right past Bar 29 to go along Millbrook. The cyclist in the foreground has a few groceries in her pannier. The little basket mounted over the front mudguard was once a very common sight in the town. These days she would have to push her bicycle over the bridge as she passed the White House pub, built on the site of a former garage in 1995, before remounting alongside another watering hole, the George Abbot. The temporary portcullis she has just ridden under is similar to one erected for the coronation celebrations in 1911. That arch rested against the walls of St Nicolas Church and the old Connaught Hotel that flanked the spot from where this photograph was taken.

Above right: This 1935 view is of the top of High Street looking down, near the junction with North Street. The arch was specially erected for the 25th anniversary of George V's accession to the throne. The roses covering the structure gave off a fragrant perfume that made passers by pause to take in their scent before moving on again. Bunting hung gaily across the street and flags flew from standards and were draped across walls. It had been a long time since the public could celebrate a monarch's silver jubilee. The last one had been in 1862 for Queen Victoria, but then rejoicing was muted as it was only a year after the death of her consort, Prince Albert. The Church of Holy Trinity is to the left of the rose arch. It holds the tomb of George Abbot, a local man who became Archbishop of Canterbury in 1611. He rose to high office from humble origins. His brother Maurice, a Lord Mayor of London, established the tomb in Holy Trinity after George's death in 1633. The tower and steeple of the original 13th century church collapsed in 1740 during alteration work. Only Abbot's tomb and the Weston family chapel survived. Rebuilding work took an age. It was not completed until 1763. Since then it has staged many important events of both local and national significance. When Guildford diocese was formed in 1927 Holy Trinity served for over 30 years as its cathedral. In 1961 the honour was transferred to the Cathedral of the Holy Spirit.

Below: Guildford's High Street used to be home to many shopkeepers as well as their place of business. Many of the concerns were family firms. The owners lived in premises over the shop. Gradually, many of these interests were replaced by the larger big name chain stores. High Street lost some of its unique quality when that happened. However, it is not all gloom and doom. The opening of the shopping malls, White Lion Walk and the Friary, attracted some of these well known names. This meant that the town was able to keep most of its individuality as some longstanding businesses retained their outlets alongside the granite setts of the High Street. In recent years financial houses have moved some of their centres to the town. Business people used to commute to London for their work. Now the reverse is often true. Who knows what they would have made of the High Street in the 19th century around Bonfire Night? It was often a real challenge to the police. The Guildford Guys regularly built a bonfire in the middle of the road and challenged the authorities to do something about it, often in the most violent of manner. Trouble was probably at its peak in the 1850s, before finally being finally quelled in 1864. These days the police have problems with guys of a different type. The number of drunks rolling along High Street or begging in the area around Eastgate Court at the upper end is a depressing sight for those with affection for the town as it was in the photograph.

Bottom: Christmas was coming in late 1956. Opposite the turning into Quarry Street White's had its trees out to mark the festive season. Elsewhere, Father Christmas had arrived in Harvey's. Mums paid their shilling so that a youngster could sit on Santa's knee. Boys got water pistols or a toy drum to thump. That really pleased the neighbours! Little girls got a magic colouring book. All they had to do was dip a brush in water and wet the page. Miraculously the water turned into paint as a work of soggy art was created. Five years before this scene was captured the Belisha beacon stood alone to indicate the pedestrian crossing. The markings on the roadway were only added in 1951 as a further aid to road safety. That was when we started calling them zebra crossings. The car parked outside Carling, Gill and Carling off licence sported an AA badge. It used to be a common sight to see a patrolman from the Automobile Association riding along on his motorbike and sidecar. He saluted the driver of any vehicle that displayed the badge. The old world courtesy was abandoned in the interests of road safety. Nealds and Cooper was once the name on the sign where Henekeys was written. Further back in time it had been the Vintners Arms. The other shops to the right belonged to a tobacconist, J Jarman, and the jeweller, R Salsbury and Sons. A short back and sides was on offer in the gents' hairdresser's above. It was topped off with a good dollop of Brylcreem.

Left: The increase in traffic on High Street was a problem even in 1938. The bypass that opened five years earlier took passing traffic away from the town, but there were still plenty of local cars to clog up the road. It was just after midday as the policeman was about to step into the road. His white armbands would be kept busy as they waved and pointed instructions to the drivers. The van belonging to Bentall's department store had come from Kingston-upon-Thames. There is now a shopping centre in that town named after the store. The restaurant on the right had a grill and tearooms, next door to the National Provincial Bank. Just before the chemist's, by the little alleyway to the right that led to North Street, the building on the corner was advertising Cossor television demonstrations. The BBC had only started transmitting pictures in 1936, so this was a real wonder of the age. However, anyone who invested in a TV set was soon to be disappointed. Broadcasts were suspended during the war. In later years a coffee house opened on the corner of the alley. It sold fresh coffee beans as well. Their aroma attracted shoppers to pause and enjoy the moment. There were also coffee shops and tearooms on the other side of High Street. Shopping was only part of the reason to come into town. It was also an opportunity to have a drink and a slice of cake whilst catching up on the latest gossip.

Above: A rainy day on Quarry Street as the coalman made his delivery. Before we all had central heating it was a common practice to watch him making his drop. The coal chute to the cellar was opened or the bunker undone. We watched him lift his cwt sacks from the lorry and empty out the black chunks of warmth. The empty sacks were laid down on the pavement or in the garden so that we could count that the right number had been delivered. What we did not check was that there was a cwt in the sack in the first place! In case younger readers are now lost, cwt stands for hundredweight. Even that is puzzling, because it means 112 lbs. Still fazed? Lbs means pounds. We had better not go further and talk of ozs. Be content that a cwt was five per cent of a ton, roughly 50 kg. Those readers who are totally metricated and cannot understand imperial measures can always take a few steps along behind where the photographer was standing. There they will find Guildford Museum, a timber framed listed building from c1630, on the corner of Castle Street. They even know about bushels and pecks in there! The church tower peeking above the trees belongs to St Mary's. The church is mainly 12th and 13th century in origin, though the tower is older. It goes back to c1040, before William I came conquering.

Bottom: The lower end of High Street falls steeply down towards the old Courts' furnishing store. From there it crosses the Wey Navigation before giving way to The Mount that climbs towards the open countryside and the Hog's Back. This view acts as a good reminder to the hilly nature of the town and its immediate environment. In 1952 we had a change of monarch, but there was no alteration to the ordinary life on Guildford's main shopping street. Half a century later and the scene is still much the same. The Angel Hotel maintains pride of place as a former coaching inn. It remains as a living souvenir of the days when posthorns sounded as great coaches hammered down the road. The undercroft opposite the Angel takes us further back in time. The stone vaulted medieval basement dates from the 13th century. The shop above was built at the start of the 19th century. In this photograph, Boot's was on the left hand side of the street, near the junction with Quarry Street. Since then it has swapped sides. It has taken over the Marks and Spencer premises. The famous department store that began life on a market stall in Leeds has moved further down the hill. Salsbury, known as the County Jeweller, had the shop below M & S. Present day Guildford has a similarly placed and named shop called Salisbury's that sells luggage and leather goods.

Right: Don't we just love a good disaster? Where there is a car crash, motorists will slow down and rubber neck to get a good look. There is always an interested crowd of onlookers at any decent factory fire. When York was devastated by flooding in November 2000 the police had to appeal to tourists to stay away because they were only coming to ogle at the water level. It was little different in the winter of 1925 when the Wey rose to epic levels and flooded the hinterland. The crowd gathered on Town Bridge, at the bottom of High Street, to watch the water race past beneath. The bridge had only been in place since the early part of the century. On 15 February 1902 the old wooden bridge, erected in 1824, suffered terminal damage when fast flowing floodwater damaged Moon's timber yard. Planks and debris were carried along in the current and smashed into the bridge with incredible force. The River Wey caused the destruction, but it had been partly responsible for Guildford's growth. It had been made navigable thanks to the ideas of Sir Richard Weston. He was the inspiration behind the introduction of 12 locks on the river in the 1650s, though he did not survive to see his plans put into practice. Sailing and horse drawn barges ferried goods along the Wey Navigation, establishing connections with London and helping Guildford's commercial growth. Some of the barges were built at Dapdune Wharf. They carried grain and gunpowder from the mills at Chilworth.

an opportunity for some historical research. The medieval foundations were uncovered. Burial grounds revealed some relics and artefacts. They gave an insight into life in the Friary before it fell foul of Henry VIII's purge of the monasteries in 1538.

Top: High Street in the late 1950s was usually much busier than this. People had money to burn. The shops were packed with customers. The pavements were crowded with shoppers anxious to buy the modern appliances that had become affordable. Perhaps this was a Sunday or early morning scene as an Austin Somerset pottered its way up towards the Guildhall. Normally, J & M Stone would have been doing a roaring trade in televisions and radiograms. The TV was no longer a luxury. It was fast becoming a fundamental piece of equipment no modern home could be without. That new phenomenon, the teenager, was opening purse and wallet to buy 78s and the newfangled 45s to put on a little Dansette record player. Mum and dad would be driven daft when Little Richard started belting out 'Tutti Frutti'. Washing machines and fridges appeared in kitchens that used to have dolly tubs and larders. The shops on this lower part of High Street that benefited from the escape from postwar austerity included Kennett, Sands' milliners, Clarke Gammon, Fremlins (under the sign with the elephant), Halfords and the Astolat tea rooms. The learner rider of the NSU Quickly moped was inside having a cuppa. He need not worry too much about his forthcoming driving test. In those days it amounted to an examiner with a clipboard standing on a street corner. You rode past, went round the block and passed him again. It was possible to fall off twice, run down a pensioner and flatten a stray tomcat. Provided all this occurred out of sight of the chap doing the testing a full licence was assured.

Above: This is a comparatively recent scene from the mid 1970s. Even so it is almost unrecognisable to anyone who came to Guildford after the Friary shopping centre was built. The complex now dominates the central area of the photograph. The Volvo to the right is a sign that times were changing. There may have been a Jaguar on the road, but the British car industry was facing increased competition from foreign manufacturers. The building in the distance is now a Witherspoon's hostelry. The old bus station became the car park for the 210 seat Electric Theatre that replaced the 1913 electricity works on Onslow Street. The shopping centre was raised on the site of the old Friary Meux brewery. There had been a number of small brewers in the town, but only the Friary remained in business after World War II. Originally formed in 1895 as the limited company of Friary Holroyd and Healy, it became Friary Meux in 1965, following a merger. Guildford brewed its last pint in 1968. The brewery was demolished in 1974. It had been built where the Dominicans once prayed. The destruction of the brewery and excavations for the foundations of the shopping centre gave archaeologists

High days & holidays

Above: Victorian women in their capes and long skirts must have found even the British summer an exhausting experience. Many wore dark clothing that absorbed the sun's rays. Tightly corseted, wasp waisted women with several layers of clothing were prone to fainting fits. It was little to do with feminine frailty and much more the result of Victorian fashion and attitude. As the float made its way up High street note the number of women who have made sure that they are standing in the shadows or are sheltering under parasols. The parade had just passed Chaplin and Co and the picture of the Queen above the legend 'Loyalty to our Queen' dates this to 20 June 1897. It was something unique in the history of the Royal Family - the Diamond Jubilee, 60 years after Victoria came to the throne. She became our monarch just weeks after her 18th birthday. She was to reign longer than any other. Other mottoes to decorate High Street included 'a record reign of light and liberty'. Neatly currycombed horses pulled the farm carts and drays used as stages to display the British way of life and our support for the monarchy. The float in the centre of the photo was passing Williamson's. This became the famous Harvey's department store, later owned by Army and Navy Stores. As 2000 came to a close it was refurbished and reopened as part of the House of Fraser.

To get a better view of the procession coming down High Street one woman and her children stood on the back of the little trap that had brought them into town. It was a good example of initiative to use the vehicle as a grandstand as well as conveyance! Colebrook's, the shop in the centre of the photograph, was a well loved seller of fish and poultry. The outside of the shop was usually covered with chickens, rabbits, hares and herrings hanging above the pavement. The gamey smells and sights had been replaced for once. Instead the proprietor demonstrated his support for the coronation celebrations of 1911. A flag was hung instead of game. A group of jugglers, stiltwalkers, street acrobats and clowns had just gone by when the banner of Holy Trinity and St Mary's Schools came into view. The boys leading the way shouldered arms as they marched along. The sight of youngsters with rifles would send shockwaves through the minds of modern sociologists. Perhaps there is something in their political correctness after all. Some of the boys would exchange their wooden guns for Lee Enfields before the 1914-18 war came to a conclusion.

Bottom: Playing cowboys and Indians is something from our childhood that looks as though it will be lost to future generations. In 1924 the stories of America's Wild West stirred the imagination of all youngsters. It had only been as recently as 1917 that William Cody died. He was better known as Buffalo Bill, hero of the plains. His touring show had been all over Europe in the early 1900s. The crowds had thrilled to the daring riding and shooting skills they saw. Real life Red Indians whooped across the arena and covered wagons were circled as they came under attack. Cowboy movies continued the public interest with that part of American history for another 50 years. Some of the parents of the 1st Merrow Scouts might have seen Buffalo Bill's show and helped inspire this tableau, called 'Indian Campfire'. These lads lived in a village that had inspired Rudyard Kipling to write about it in his 1902 'Just So Stories'. 'There runs a road by Merrow Down, a grassy track today it is, an hour out of Guildford town.' He must have been a slow walker! When Kipling wrote about the village it had a population of only just over 1,300. Merrow became part of Guildford in 1933. It kept some of its independent way of life, but suffered the indignity of having Merrow Road renamed Epsom Road. The scouts on the float would be sad to know that modern do-gooders dislike little boys playing with guns. Cowboys and native Americans might be politically correct, but it does not have the same ring to it as the old name had. Younger readers might like to know that the author, Kipling, did not make exceedingly good cakes!

Right: After over 63 years of Queen Victoria's reign the nation celebrated two coronations within a short time at the beginning of the 20th century. Edward VII was crowned in 1902. He succeeded his mother when he was nearly 60, the oldest of our monarchs to accede to the throne. When he died on 6 May 1910 his second son, George Frederick Ernest Albert, became George V. His coronation took place on 22 June 1911 and was the reason for these celebrations. Floats, brightly decked out with flowers, flags and pretty drapes, formed a procession through the town. This tableau was entitled 'Triumph and Peace'. The sea dragon represented Britain's naval power. Our men of war dominated the seas, guaranteeing that their strong presence would ensure peace or could conquer all adversity. Little did we know what was to unfold across the world in three years' time. In 1911 George V headed the largest Empire in the world. At his coronation the guests included premiers of dominion countries and Indian princes wearing jewelled turbans and clothes of gold. On the blue carpets of Westminster Abbey, flanked by banks of red tulips, white lilies and blue delphiniums, he was crowned 'King of the United Kingdom of Great Britain and Ireland and of the British Dominions beyond the seas, Defender of the Faith, Emperor of India'. Wow! How could the shooting of some Austro-Hungarian Archduke in Sarajevo in 1914 possibly disturb such power and might?

This page: The Silver Jubilee processions of 1935 gave various groups and organisations the chance to advertise their existence or membership. Some traders used the opportunity for subtle advertising. However, most people in the procession just enjoyed taking part. There were many tableaux and floats for the crowd to admire. Lowloaders and lorry backs were pressed into use by scouts and guides. Pretty girls who had won competitions sat on makeshift thrones and hung onto their crowns and sashes as the trail led along Stoke Road. The jolly mixture of streamers, balloons, bathing belles and lifebelts belonged to the swimming club from Guildford Lido, on the edge of Stoke Park. The open air pool with its diving boards was an immediate hit when it opened in the summer of 1933. The adventure of mixed bathing was attractive to all but the oldfashioned and prudish. The little ones enjoyed the paddling pool and the café was always busy serving teas, as it still does today. Families spent whole days there, bringing picnics to share on the extensive grassy areas. The attractive fountains lent the scene a nice artistic touch. The Lido underwent a major £1 million facelift in 1998. We can thank

William Harvey, owner of the prestigious department store that linked High Street and North Street for the Lido. It was only right that Mayor Harvey should perform the opening ceremony as he was instrumental in its creation. It was his plan to use the 1932 Work Fund to finance the venture. This was a scheme whereby local people gave weekly contributions to help the unemployed during the depression years. The building of the Lido provided employment for 600 men. The mayor stripped off his robes after the opening ceremony to reveal a natty pair of trunks. He executed the first dive seen at the Lido. Although not compulsory, most of his successors have followed in his footsteps at the start of each summer season. Harvey was later awarded the OBE and given the freedom of the borough.

The soccer player on his float was representing Guildford City FC. At one time the town boasted two well known outfits. Guildford FC (the Pinks) was an amateur club of some note. It was founded in 1877 and played at Woodbridge Road, but folded in 1953. The better known club that was based at Josephs Road was formed in 1921 as Guildford United. To mark the creation of Guildford diocese and the raising of the Church of Holy Trinity to cathedral status, in 1927 the club changed its name to Guildford City. One of its top stars around 1930 was Ronnie Rooke. He went on to play top flight football for the mighty Arsenal and Fulham. City won the Southern League in 1937-38, a feat it repeated in 1955-56. Its name was on the Southern League Cup in 1963 and 1967. Just a handful short of 10,000 crammed into Josephs Road in 1938 to witness a thrilling first round FA Cup replay against Aldershot. The midweek match saw countless grannies having funerals as people took time off work to watch City lose an epic encounter 4-3. It was a sad day for local sport when the club was wound up in 1974. Soon the place was derelict and the grandstand destroyed when vandals set fire to it. The land was developed for housing in 1977.

Above: These sweet violets of the 1924 carnival included one who was true to the description. Violet Hayes is the young woman with the beautiful smile, second left. What a charmer she looked. The boys would have been turning weak at the knees when she twinkled her eyes and flashed those pearly white teeth their way. By her side is Mrs Hayes, presumably her mother. Mum and daughter were flanked left and right by Beryl Mursell and Muriel Johnson. The Christian names are right for the time. They were as popular as Tracey and Sharon became 60 years later. It is also typical of the era that newspaper reports carried the Christian names of the young women but not of the married one. It was thought to be too invasive of her privacy. Anyway, she had surrendered her real name when she was taken on as the wife of Mr Hayes. No wonder the Suffragettes got their way. Mrs Hayes had probably worked her fingers to the bone raising Violet all through the 1914-18 war, supported the war effort by sacrificing her pots and pans for warships and carried out a job vacated by the men who had gone to war. She did all that whilst keeping body and soul together in the family home. Despite that she remained semi anonymous behind her husband's surname and, usually, his initials as well.

Above right: Guildford has always loved a good carnival. It has been a popular way for people to celebrate events or simply just to publicise the delights of the town. On 17 September 1924 lorry backs and lowloaders were pressed into service as floats. Their cabs and sides were festooned with flowers. Streamers floated gaily in the breeze and

attractive garlands were hung from every quarter of each float. Carnival queens and rose princesses proudly took their places on their thrones. Tableaux depicting historical scenes or those reflecting the modern age competed side by side. Others were used by businesses or interest groups to get their message across. Although firms got some publicity from advertising their wares, the main purpose of joining in the carnival procession was to show some community spirit. This Co-operative Society float had a message for a wider community. How true it was. Only six years before the world had just returned to some sanity when the Great War ended. It was by co-operating with our allies that we were victorious. The war had been won. Now it was time to win the peace. The message would have been over the heads of the little ones taking part in the procession. Sadly, they would understand it 15 years later when their husbands and sweethearts left them and, in many cases, never came back. But those days were too far ahead to trouble these girls. They just wanted to enjoy this moment and who could deny them that pleasure?

The 1924 carnival float had come to rest on York Road, opposite Sandfield Terrace. The children had been brushed and scrubbed for their part in the day's festivities. Their mothers took a pride ion seeing them turned out so well. The adults' formal and dour look is so different from the bright colours and variety of styles that we can see in the 21st century. Women would not be seen dead out of doors unless they were wearing a hat. Nor did many men go bareheaded. They also wore jackets and trousers, because these were the clothes for an occasion. Whether it was a carnival or a night out, overalls and work clothes were not appropriate. Perhaps the float had paused for a moment so that the menfolk could pop into the Elm Tree. It certainly would not have been thought right if their wives did so. They had to stay outside and mind the children. Formerly the Old Elm Tree, the pub had been built on land where the militia used to drill. As might be expected from the name, there had once been an avenue of trees here that led down to the old Dominican friary. There had been a large elm tree left in place when the pub opened for the first time, but it was badly damaged in the severe thunderstorms of 1906 that also flooded the beer cellars. The Elm Tree's first landlord, Robert Downes, started serving customers in 1887. Well over a century later it is still a popular haunt for locals. However, nowadays the women are allowed to come inside without fear of criticism.

CO-OPERATION STANDS FOR THE PEACE OF THE WORLD

Left: These children were representing all the home countries of the United Kingdom. They had been carefully prepared in national dress, with a few extra frills to make the point. There was even a lad dressed as a soldier of the King, beating a drum as he proudly displayed the standard. We are witnessing the occasion of the sixth annual dance of the Corona School of Dancing, held in the assembly room at Brett's restaurant. These precious tots tapped away in their special shoes or tiptoed in their ballet wear as they practised with a dedication worthy of a professional. At the dance they put on routines for doting mums and dads. There were Irish jigs and Highland flings. The high hats of the Welsh girls whirled as madly as the bodies underneath and the English demonstrated folk dances that were popular in rural village squares up and down the land. Everyone joined in with the Cumberland reel and the Scottish sword dance. They even had a go at the Gay Gordons and cheered those who pointed their toes and wiggled them from front to back like little leprechauns. In 1925 we had a pride in being part of Great Britain. Cardiff, Belfast, Edinburgh and Guildford were all part of a nation that pulled together. We recognised each other's customs and were happy to share and celebrate them. These happy children, now well into their 80s, must regret that our country has started dividing itself up into fragments by having separate political assemblies.

Above: The cattle market on Woodbridge Road was held on a weekly basis. It had taken place in the High Street until 1865 when it moved to North Street. It came to Woodbridge Road in 1896, where it stayed until its removal to Slyfield Green in 1969. Guildford was also given the ancient right to hold two annual fairs. From 1341 there was a May Fair devoted largely to sheep and horses. The Winter Fair in November was a smaller occasion and became more of an entertainment fair. By the 1920s it had become little more than an annual Woodbridge Road funfair. But, these laden Daimlers were not connected with trading animal flesh. Their cargo was human. Noisy and excited, but definitely human. It was 30 June 1924 and they were off to visit the British Empire Exhibition at Wembley. The outing for 500 children from the elementary schools would be repeated on 7 July when another contingent headed off to the stadium that had captured the public imagination the previous year. That was when a policeman on a white horse had helped clear crowds so that the FA Cup Final could go ahead. The exhibition had opened on 23 April by telegram. King George V sent an electric message to himself from London via Canada, New Zealand, Australia, South Africa, India, Egypt and Gibraltar. It raced right round the world. The telegram was handed to his majesty in front of 50,000 people just 80 seconds after he sent it. The opening ceremony was listened to by 6,000,000, thanks to the BBC.

Above: The skipper of the Sandford Junior Technical School held the shield the side had won during the 1924-25 season. It was presented in July 1925 to the school as champions of the Guildford Borough Schools League. School sport was very important for most of the 20th century. It helped youngsters exercise and enjoy the bonding of team games. The players were proud to represent their school. The teachers gained pleasure in the pupils' achievements. They gave their time after school and on Saturday mornings. It was simply part of the job. So it continued until union action in the mid 1980s and the administrative demands of the National Curriculum scuppered a lot of school sport and other outdoor activities. Sometimes people poked fun at the teachers who, like Brian Glover in the film 'Kes', lived out a fantasy on the sports field. But, without their contribution, present day schools have lost a lot. The Sandford team might have included one boy who was useless academically. Yet, he starred as a footballer. That was worth a great deal for his self esteem. The school team played its heart out in conditions that would make today's players wince. The leather ball weighed a ton when it was wet. Many is the time that a centre half collapsed with concussion after a series of headed clearances. He was revived with a cold sponge and told to get on with it. When the final whistle went there was time to sneak a look at the girls on the hockey field nearby before going back to a draughty changing room.

Above right: Just look at the sensible shoes and boots these students were wearing. They did not come to school in fancy flashing trainers. They wore practical footwear for the walk to school through the snow and the rain. These girls were not like the wimps of today, ferried to and from the school gates by car. The pupils of the Charlottesville Board School were made of sterner stuff. They were also a skilful set of youngsters. They had just won the Watkin needlework competition. The

examiners described the work as 'the best in the history of the competition'. The headmaster, Mr Gardiner, stood proudly by the group that had beaten all comers to win the 1926 competition. They had to wait until March 1927 to receive it, but E Edwards on the front row held it proudly for all to admire. Mr Gardiner looks to have been a young headmaster. Perhaps it is a sign of our advancing years when bobbies and school principals look youthful! It is not certain what role Miss Gaines, on the right, had played. Perhaps she had taught the girls the art of embroidery, crochet and needlecraft. The children included crewel work, petit point, cross-stitch embroidery and quilting amongst their talents. These would come in useful when they got older, both as a hobby and for practical purposes. These were times when women made clothes for the family, used knitting patterns and ran up curtains. Be honest, when was the last time you ever darned a sock? Miss Gaines would be ashamed of you.

Right: The Picture Palace had a complete change of programme every Monday and Thursday. 'Clothes', featuring Olive Tell and 'Sauce for the goose' from the Gaumont Film Hire Service were being advertised to encourage people to pass through the doors. Smartly suited commissionaires waited at the entrance on Onslow Street to welcome customers. One of them must have been very young, to tell from the empty pushchair on the pavement. Perhaps the baby had been 'Saved from the sea' by Nora Swinbourne, as the billboard on the wall behind might have been suggesting. An added treat in store was on its way on Thursday. Eddie Polo, the king of the clowns, was on his way. The style of entertainment has changed dramatically since the days of the early cinema. In the 1920s audiences watched steamy scenes played out by that great screen lover Rudolph Valentino in such silent epics as 'The Sheikh'. All this was performed to the accompaniment of a cinema pianist or organist. Mood music heightened the tension or lightened the romance. In 1926 hysterical women wept for days when Valentino died aged just 31. When Hollywood had its great days with the early talkies in the 1930s, women copied the hair styles and clothing fashions worn by stars like Joan Crawford and Rosalind Russell. In the 1960s, when many cinemas lost custom to television, the Picture Palace became a dance hall called the Plaza. Later still 'clickety click' and 'Kelly's eye' rang out from the bingo caller. It is now a nightclub.

Below: The Theatre Royal stood on North Street on the opposite corner of Leapale Road from the Congregational Church. The church also boasted a popular Sunday school next door to it. It was so highly recommended that even Anglicans attended it! This side of North Street had some fine architecture. A series of structures, all built in a Gothic style from local stone, once made this area an imposing sight. Nowadays we only have Index and the Early Learning Centre to look at. It is hardly a fair exchange. The Theatre Royal opened in 1912. The building was formerly the County and Borough Halls. Variety and music hall acts were popular, especially with people who lived in such areas as provided by the Caxton Housing Scheme or the council at Shepherd's Hill, Stoughton. These halls were the breeding grounds for many of the future top stars of entertainment. Here they practised their art in front of audiences who were both demanding and supportive. A good turn got rapturous applause, but a poor show got the bird. There was a variety of acts to suit all tastes. Most would do two spots, either side of the interval. Singers and comedians were commonplace. There were also dancers, animal acts, mindreaders, jugglers and acrobats. A comic could have an act that was taken around the country without any need to change the script until he returned to a venue the following year. Local and touring shows, like the Henley Revue, often came as a package. Jack Smiles and Dandy George are stage names belonging to that age and style of variety show. The Theatre Royal closed in 1932 because it breached fire safety regulations.

Bird's eye view

Memories of **GUILDFORD**

First mention of Guildford as a settlement was made in about 880 AD when it was developing as a major defensive and commercial centre in Surrey. The three main roads at the time were North street, High Street and Castle Street. The castle, at the bottom, is the only Norman one to be built in the county. The windows, let into the walls of the keep, date from the Tudor period. Henry III granted Guildford its Royal Charter in 1256. In the following century Edward III invited Flemish weavers to the town. They helped establish Guildford's importance as a wool town, a position it maintained until the 18th century. This 1967 view shows how North Street and High Street continued to dominate as the town's focal points. They run across the lower centre of the picture. Chertsey Street snakes up and away from its junction with North Street. From there we can make out some of the buildings of the Royal Grammar School. Its old building goes back to the 16th century. Allen House Gardens lie behind the modern school buildings. Its tennis courts, bowling green and putting green were laid in the gardens of the house that was demolished in 1964 to make way for the school's expansion. Sydenham Road multi storey car park is the white building in the foreground. The cricket ground in the distance hosted occasional visits from Surrey CC, when the batsmanship of John Edrich, Mickey Stewart and Ken Barrington entertained the crowds.

Above: The Wey floods quite regularly. In mid September 1968 Guildford was subjected to nearly four inches of rain in just 24 hours. The river is towards the top of the photograph, but there were places where it was difficult to see where its real banks were. The lower High Street, out of picture to the left, was under six feet of water. Car parks and the cattle market resembled lakes. This part of town shows Woodbridge Road, Commercial Road and Onslow Street. They lead towards St Saviour's Church, at the bottom right of the photograph. Walnut Tree Close hugs the far bank of the Wey, with the railway line just above it. Both the river and the railway were important in Guildford's development. The Wey Navigation, now controlled by the National Trust, was one of the first of Britain's navigable waterways. Before the days of the great canal builders of the early Industrial Revolution era, the Wey Navigation led the way. It opened in 1651, linking the Wey to the Thames. It also enhanced the town's importance as a market town. The corn trade was particularly important. Guildford was the market centre for much of west Surrey. When the railway was established, nearly 200 years later, its future as the county town was assured. Since this aerial shot was taken the new gyratory road system has changed the face of this part of town. Today's photographer would capture rush hour traffic fighting its way in and out of town on busy highways.

Right: Looking north across the centre of the town, the main shopping areas of High Street and North Street run across the picture. This was 1966, the year when the country had a decent football team. The castle can be seen at the bottom of the photograph. These are the remains of a late 12th century tower keep. The Norman castle was built c1170 in Bargate stone. The neatly kept gardens are a pleasant place to relax, away from the hurly burly of the town. Schoolchildren learnt to swim in the baths on Castle Street. In the late 1950s and early 1960s there was a coffee bar on the first floor of the building near to Tunsgate Arch, to the right centre of the photograph. Boxer's was an example that even Guildford could not avoid the youth culture. Teenagers quaffed frothy coffee and Coca Cola to the sounds of Lonnie Donegan, Nancy Whiskey and the Vipers skiffle music. The songs of the similarly named Marty Wilde, Billy Fury and Vince Eagar then superseded that fad. Towards the top of the picture the pointed turret of the old fire station, on the corner of Ward Street and North Street, reaches heavenwards. Guildford Institute is on the opposite corner of Ward Street. It was built in 1892 as the Guildford and Working Men's Institute. Now a part of the university, it houses a Victorian library and hosts a number of cultural activities.

In 1970, when the bottom end of the town was photographed, Guildford was about to embark on a period of change. Older buildings would be swept away and a new era of shopping malls and road systems was on its way. Debenhams' large store, close to the Town Bridge, had already arrived. Little girls used to get their toys mended at the dolls' hospital on Swan Lane, near where the White Lion Walk shopping centre now stands. The repertory theatre, with such leading lights as Christopher Guinee, had, since 1946, provided entertainment on the corner of Leapale Road and North Street. However, its demise could not be blamed on the developers. It was ravaged by fire in 1963. Interest turned to the construction of the riverside Yvonne Arnaud theatre, out of camera to the right of Debenhams. In the centre of this 1970 scene we still had the delightful steeple of the Methodist Church. Lower down, the old bus station and Friary brewery would give way to the developers. The Electric Theatre and a car park replaced the former. The brewery was flattened to make way for the Friary shopping centre. The curved building close to the junction of Woodbridge Road and Commercial Road belonged to Angel, Son and Gray. James Angel came from Wales in 1889 and established an ironmongery business. The company expanded to the degree that this part of town was known as Angel's Corner.

Building a reputation

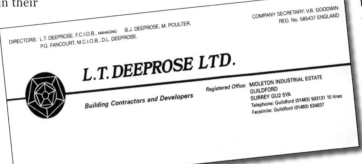

According to the old adage an Englishman's home is his castle. That may be only metaphorically true but the phrase makes more than a dubious legal point. Our homes are important to us whether we live in the smallest of flats or the largest mansion. People take pride in their homes no matter what their circumstances and that pride in possession and occupation must have existed since our ancestors painted their bodies with woad and lived in huts made of wattle and daub or of stones and turf. And if our ancestors could take such pride in their simple homes how much more pride we today should feel about our modern houses, flats and bungalows.

But of course homes must be built by someone. In the years since the end of the second world war thousands of new homes have been built in Britain to accommodate an ever-increasing population and to replace the many old and substandard buildings hastily erected during the Victorian era. The area in and around Guildford, like most of the south of England, has seen remarkable changes in the last fifty years or so, changes which are still continuing before our eyes. The rural and urban landscape has been transformed by the many high quality homes which have been built in those years, and one firm which has contributed more than most to those changes has been the Guildford firm of building contractors and developers L T Deeprose Ltd.

Founded in 1947 by Leslie T Deeprose the Deeprose Company has progressed from small beginnings to become one of the region's foremost construction companies with an annual turnover now approaching 10 million pounds.

Since its early days the company has always been a presence in contracting and housing and has in the intervening years established a reputation for high quality together with economy and successful completion on time.

The story of the Deeprose Company is of course very much that of its founder and Chairman, Leslie Deeprose.

Leslie Deeprose was born in London and brought up in Sydenham before his parents moved to Guildford in 1936. In 1943 at the age of 18 young Leslie joined the RAF serving as a Flight Engineer on Lancaster bombers at Mildenhall in Suffolk, Tuddenham and Mepal near Ely.

After completing his War service in May 1947 Leslie returned to his family home, a semi in Cherry Tree Avenue on the Bannisters Farm estate opposite the Cathedral. Leslie's father had bought the semi in 1936 for the then princely sum of £495 - a significant amount for his father, an engineer in a leather factory, to find when the average weekly wage in those days was just £2.50.

DIRECTORS: L.T. DEEPROSE, F.C.I.O.B., MANAGING   B.J. DEEPROSE, M. POULTER.
P.G. FANCOURT, M.C.I.O.B., D.L. DEEPROSE.

COMPANY SECRETARY: V.B. GOODWIN
REG. No. 585437 ENGLAND

L.T. DEEPROSE LTD.

Building Contractors and Developers

Registered Office: MIDLETON INDUSTRIAL ESTATE
GUILDFORD
SURREY GU2 5YA
Telephone: Guildford (01483) 503131 10 lines
Facsimile: Guildford (01483) 534837

Top left: *Leslie Deeprose pictured during his time in the RAF.* **Above:** *An early letterhead.*
Right: *Norman Payne, Mrs Mary Lloyd-Jones and Leslie Deeprose at the handover of five new houses in Pound Field, Guildford.*

Before being called up Leslie had worked for the firm of Dennis Bros and been involved in maintenance work, undertaking plumbing and pipe fitting amongst other tasks. After his return to civvy street times were hard. Leslie's wife Barbara was ill but many local people wanted to help him by finding a few jobs for him to do to keep him going until he found a 'proper job'. Those small jobs involved plumbing and minor general electrical work and through those small jobs he was eventually put in touch with Harry Edmead, a local jobbing builder, who carried considerable local credit as a churchgoer and pillar of the local community.

So Leslie got on his bike, carrying his bag of tools, and went to work for Harry Edmead on an ad-hoc basis. That part time, one off work, soon led to him being employed almost continuously. Because he was too busy Leslie needed better transport than a bike and soon bought a van - a 1930 Morris Minor which had previously been used as a fish delivery van. The van cost just £15 and was in a sad condition but he rebuilt and repainted it. Later he acquired an old taxi from a scrap yard, a Hillman Wizard, and cut the back off to make a truck for his work.

Although most of Leslie's work was coming from Harry Edmead he was building his own reputation too. Private work came in and he began employing a carpenter, and then another, moving up from jobbing plumbing to small kitchen and bathroom extensions. Leslie soon needed a joinery workshop and found one in Walnut Tree Close where most of

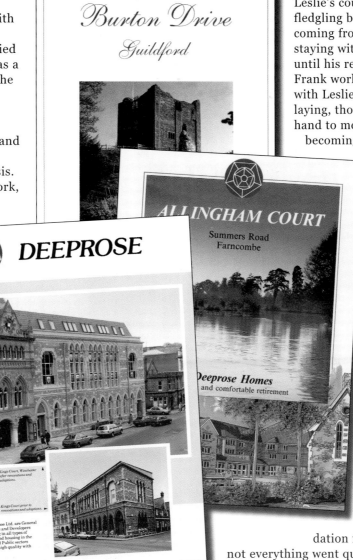

Above: *Brochures on various properties renovated or built by the company.*

the woodworking was done. Looking for more business he made representations to various local estate agents and luckily found a regular source of work through the firm of Moldram, Clarke and Edgley doing property maintenance. Leslie also found a close friend there, Mr Maurice Edgley of the estate agents, a friendship which lasted until Mr Edgley's death in 1997.

In 1949 Frank Wakefield, Leslie's cousin, joined the fledgling building firm, coming from London and staying with the company until his retirement in 1989. Frank worked side by side with Leslie and took up bricklaying, though he turned his hand to most things, quickly becoming not only a mainstay of the firm but also a Director in 1957 when the business became a Limited Company.

During those early years Leslie's wife Barbara was a pillar of support for her husband helping with the office work and telephones. In 1950 Leslie had the opportunity to build a bungalow at Farley Heath for a farmer who needed accommodation for his staff. But not everything went quite as smoothly as he might have wished; he had to sack a plumber who, on discovering that a heating element was too long, simply sawed it to length!

All this time, Leslie had been running his business from home, a council house in Bellfieds estate. After the Farley Heath job he continued with alteration and extension work until 1952 when he bought land at Jacobs Well on which to build five bungalows: the land cost £1,000 plus £30 in solicitors fees. The Jacobs Well project went well and the fifth bungalow he built for himself; the other four he sold for £2,400 each. This was the start of house building for Deeprose. By the following year eight tradesmen were being employed.

Going on from the Jacobs Well scheme Leslie built several private houses throughout an area of 15 miles around Guildford. The culture of the business at that time was simple 'never refuse a job' and he took on whatever work he was offered - anything which would make a profit.

The firm became a limited company , L T Deeprose Ltd, on 12 June 1957 with Leslie and his cousin Frank Wakefield as Directors.

A Mrs Potter was employed as the very first secretary/book keeper in an office in the bungalow at Jacobs Well. Mr Edgley of Moldram Clarke and Edgley introduced Leslie to a vacant plot of land in Queens Road, Guildford which was taken on and the company built a two storey office, the firm's first purpose built premises. The company moved there in 1958 and would stay there until 1973.

By the early 1960s projects involving five or six houses soon became 12 and 15 houses and would, much later, become schemes of up to 100 homes.

In 1965 at the age of 19 Derek Deeprose joined his father in the company; his first duties were to service the various sites the company worked on with plant and material.

In 1969 Peter Fancourt joined as an estimator/surveyor and soon proved his worth as a member of the team and in 1984 both Derek and Peter became directors. Today Peter is responsible for all estimates submitted and is known for his particular skill on obtaining clear and economical solutions on design and build opportunities.

Above left: *A 1928 Austin 12/4 heavy chassis restored in the company's workshop.*
Above right: *Company vehicles showing the contrasting livery between yesteryear and today.*
Below: *Paul Deeprose during his apprenticeship.*

Derek and Frank set up a Small Works department for the company. Later they moved on to major contracts, Frank as contracts manager and Derek as site Agent.

Joe Blacketer joined the company as small works manager and the small works department took care of all projects costing up to £150,000 and Joe proved himself to be an extremely competent manager, and became a director in 1980. The department went from strength to strength under his guidance; he was well known and well liked by colleagues and customers alike and the company still believe the likes of Joe will never be seen again in the industry. Joe was ably assisted in the small works department by Graham Ford as assistant manager: Graham is still with the company today.

Meanwhile large projects continued: in 1972 for example the company built the C of E school at Haslemere. In 1973 a four storey block of flats in Godalming became the first project the company did involving concrete piles for foundations; a significant progression for a small building company.

The firm acquired its current premises on Guildford's Midleton Industrial Estate in 1973 after negotiating a land lease with Guildford Borough Council whereupon the company built a two storey office block, joiners shop and yard. Later a third storey and wing extension were added. The deal for the premises was made by Mike Poulter who had joined the company as a surveyor and who was to

become a company director in 1974, eventually serving as Leslie's right hand man for many years. Today Mike Poulter is Senior Director and is responsible for all surveying matters and the company's maintenance team ensuring customer satisfaction during defects periods and maintaining contact with existing clients.

Another stalwart was Gerry Stemp who set up the accounts department and was in charge of computerising accounts; he became company secretary in 1974 remaining so until his retirement in 1993, whilst by the millennium another stalwart, David Payne, the company buyer had clocked up over 20 years with the firm.

Amongst the major projects completed by the firm during those years was the sports hall and teaching block at Yeomans Bridge School in Ash in 1977 whilst a new science block at the Godalming Sixth Form college followed three years later.

In 1974 the company embarked on a project which could easily have led to its demise. The scheme involved the speculative buying of land from John Kidd and Andrew Sturt - building on the site was a challenge involving a concrete frame on a steep slope. The flats at West Mount took four years to complete rather than the projected two and by the end of it, due to a housing market depression, the company was selling the flats at a loss. Leslie had planned to sell the 35 units of two and three

Above: *King's Court, Winchester after renovations.*

bedroomed flats for at least £18,995 per unit but ended up selling at £12,550, well below cost. By sheer grit and determination the company survived partly by extending the building period and concentrating on the contracting side of the business to support it and partly by persuading the bank to support them. Today Leslie Deeprose is rueful to note that the West Mount flats he built which so nearly broke the company are now changing hands for £260,000 each.

Inspired by misplaced confidence in the profitability of the West Mount project in 1978 the top floor was added to the company offices. Had the company known the problems it would face the extension might have been delayed. In the longer term however more expansion would eventually follow when the wing extension was added in 1984.

Despite its problems the firm survived to take on more major projects: Henry Reeve provided a site at Tilehouse, Guildford, for four blocks of 48 retirement flats with a community centre. On completion the £800,000 scheme was handed over to a housing association and named Reeve Court. Another major project in that period was at the Bramley Grange Hotel where a wing of retirement flats were built adjoining the hotel - although sadly the hotel was subsequently burnt down as a result of a fire in the hotel kitchens. 43 flats were built at Springside Court, Guildford, 29 at Lady Place Court, Alton and 49 flats and five houses at Allingham Court, Farncombe. 26 houses were built at Grange Road in Guildford, now known as Deeprose Close and many other smaller projects involving between one and fifteen houses were

completed. The company would eventually build nearly 1,000 homes around Guildford. Employees tend to make a career with L T Deeprose; Bob Fox for example who joined the company in 1983 to promote house building and the development of land. In 1989 his skills were realigned to include design and build contracts particularly for housing associations and to prepare sketches for all the company's developments: today Bob is the firm's development manager.

L T Deeprose is a true family business; employees have tended to stay with the company earning long service benefits and staying until eventual retirement. Joe Blacketer for example who had been in charge of Small Works retired only in 1992 and shortly afterwards emigrated to Australia where Leslie still keeps in touch with him. From then on however the Small Works department struggled without Joe's particular brand of management and it subsequently incurred losses. A board decision was made to wind down Small Works and the department was eventually closed. Today the company no longer takes in work of less than £500,000 in value.

Leslie's grandson, Paul Deeprose, joined the company as an apprentice joiner on leaving school at the age of 16. He completed his apprenticeship as a first class craftsman and was made assistant site foreman and, gaining more responsibility, came into the company office as assistant contracts manager and within weeks had proved his worth and

Below: *West Mount, Guildford.*

quickly became a contracts manager. Today Paul is responsible for £12 million of work along with Pat McMahon the first Construction manager. Pat joined the company in the early 1980s and today is responsible for completion of contracts on time and within budget.

Val Goodwin, Leslie's daughter, joined the family firm in April 1986 as Mike Poulter's PA eventually taking over as Company Secretary. Today she keeps overall control of the administration and smooth running of office functions.

Other new names include Drahomira Vidal who took over from Gerry Stemp as accounts manager and she keeps overall control of the company's finances.

The company can look back with pride at its many major projects including the Vanbrugh Suite at the Yvonne Arnaud Theatre, the domestic science block at Guildford Girls High School, the PACE centre at

Above: *Renovation works to a Sussex Barn in Aldershot to provide Design Studios.*

Guildford Police Station, the kitchens and dining rooms at HM Coldingley Prison at Bisley, the Magnetic Imaging Centre at the Royal Surrey Hospital and several refurbishment contracts in and around Guildford Town Centre. Projects have ranged from an extension and refurbishment of Guildford Golf Club at a cost of over half a million pounds to the other end of the scale where the company has built 100 houses at Bracklesham Bay in West Sussex at a cost of almost £4 million completing that project in just 78 weeks.

John Robinson came in as Chief Executive in 1999 accountable to Leslie Deeprose: his brief was to maintain the company's position as a regional contractor and to develop the firm's client base in both the public and private sectors. Before coming to Deeprose John had over 25 years experience in the industry both locally and nationally and has committed himself to the long term development of the company. John Robinson became a director of L T Deeprose in 2000 and since his arrival the company's emphasis has been on redefining its role within the industry concentrating on strengths built up over seven decades. Today the company offers Clients a full range of services including joint venture developments, design and build schemes, partnering, competitive tendering, budget pricing, negotiated contracts, construction management, major refurbishments and specialist services.

This has provided a shift in the size of Contract resulting in the Company's current projects having an average size in excess of £1 million. The client base and type of contract have also changed.

Above: *Juliet House, Godalming.*
Top: *Lindsey House, Addlestone.*

The Company is going through a period of change whereby it expects to evolve to meet the rigours of development and contracting in the twenty first century without turning its back on either its roots, or the clients who have helped it attain the profitable position it finds itself in today.

The story of Leslie Deeprose and the Company he founded is one which Guildford can be proud of. The fact that a major company can grow from such tiny beginnings is a lasting tribute to its founder, a reflection on the dedication of his workforce over many decades and an inspiration to others who might hope to follow the same path. All landscapes change over time, sometimes the change is for the better sometimes for the worse. The Deeprose commitment to quality has ensured that where new buildings have been constructed they have been in harmony with our heritage and have provided us with buildings and homes we can feel even more proud of than our ancestors did of their castle, huts and cottages in that long gone England of yesteryear.

Guildford Borough Council appointed the Company to build a sheltered housing scheme in East Horsley and private client PMB Holdings Ltd have negotiated a hi-tech office/industrial development in South Wimbledon, both projects with a value in excess of £2 million.

The rest of the current workload provides a full cross-section of projects for both Public and Private Clients with around 50 per cent of all work procured on a negotiated basis.

Due to prudent management the business has a strong financial base. The company aims to combine the best of traditional crafts with modern equipment and management techniques to provide the right quality of construction at the most economical cost to clients. The firm's proven success is based on the experience and ability of staff and the craftsmen employed to meet the highest standards and whilst 'design and build' constitutes the major part of the firm's workload it continues to carry out contracts by traditional procurement methods working regularly with external consultants.

Top: *Construction under way on the 42,000sq ft office and industrial premises at the Observatory, South Wimbledon.* ***Above:*** *The recently completed sheltered accommodation complex at St Martin's Court, East Horsley.* ***Below:*** *Leslie and Barbara Deeprose celebrate the company's 50th Anniversary.*

Events & occasions

The flags were out and they were waved with great gusto. On 30 April 1924 the Duke and Duchess of York were driven along High Street through the massed ranks of cheering crowds who braved the foul weather to mark their position as loyal subjects. The couple came to Guildford to perform the opening ceremony for the new outpatients' wing at the County Hospital. Originally called the Royal Surrey County Hospital, it opened in April 1866. It was built on Farnham Road with £17,000 of money from public subscription. The hospital replaced Guildford Dispensary in Quarry Street. It had only opened in 1859, but, originally, the new hospital was built to be the general hospital for the whole of the county, not just the town. The 60 bed building was

dedicated to the memory of Prince Albert, husband of Queen Victoria, who died in 1861. It became a charitable hospital for the sick poor. A nurses' home, designed by Edward Lunn, was opened in 1908. When an addition was to be made to the hospital it seemed fitting that a senior figure of royalty should come and perform the opening ceremony, considering the subject of its original dedication. From 1928, until the birth of the NHS in 1948, it was operated under a contributory scheme known as the West Surrey and Aldershot Hospitals League. How many of the crowd cheering the royal visitors on their way along High Street would still be around 76 years later when Queen Elizabeth the Queen Mother, as the Duchess was to become, celebrated her personal centenary?

Below: They crammed together like so many sardines in a John West tin. The rain lashed down, but the onlookers turned smiling faces towards the camera to record forever their attendance at the outpatients' wing of the County Hospital. They had not come for treatment, which was just as well because thousands thronged the building. The crowds were there to bear witness to the opening ceremony. They had come to catch a glimpse of royalty. It was not an opportunity to be missed. In modern times we have had television, video and film that have brought the Royal Family into our homes with such frequency that such images are commonplace. This photograph was taken at a time when there was still a mystique about figures of high birth or important station. When they came to town for some official function people just had to see them in the flesh. On went the homburgs. Flat caps were rammed onto heads. High crowned hats with wide brims that shaded the eyes were carefully put in place. Up went the umbrellas and they were ready to face the elements and cheer the visitors who graced the occasion. Those who

could not get a good view perched on top of railings and fences. People living nearby hung out of windows. A royal visit was an occasion that brought the population onto the street to wave the flag. What did a little dampness matter? They were in the presence of greatness.

Bottom: She was the best loved member of all the Royal Family in the 20th century and, yet, she was not our monarch. That natural smile warmed the hearts of everyone who met her, young and old, rich and poor. She was born Lady Elizabeth Bowes-Lyon, daughter of the 14th Earl of Strathmore. We grew to know her in the second half of the century as the 'Queen Mum'. That winning smile immediately captivated the hearts of the general public when she came to its attention the previous year on 26 April 1923 when she married Albert, Duke of York. He was the second son of George V. As a descendant of Robert the Bruce she was a true Brit. This broke the mould of foreign princesses marrying in to the Royal Family. It was less than five years since the war

with Germany and a home grown wife for the future George VI was a popular choice. At the time people did not know that her husband would accede to the throne when his brother abdicated in 1936, so making her Queen Consort. They were just happy to see such a charming royal representative supporting her husband at the opening ceremony of the new wing of the County Hospital. She made the dignitaries feel special when she warmly accepted the greeting of the members of the council lined up for her to meet. Amongst their number that day were the town clerk, RC Knight, and Aldermen Rapkins, Baker, Phillips and Franks. The 'Queen Mum' celebrated her 100th birthday on 4 August 2000. She was still smiling then.

Above: In recent times we have had political pundits and experts talking us through general elections. Television audiences have got used to Robin Day or David Dimbleby leading discussion programmes. There have been Bob McKenzie and Peter Snow with swingometers and wondrous graphs and charts. Exit polls try to tell us the result within minutes of the end of polling. It takes some of the magic of surprise out of the equation. What could be more fun than the nonsense of the American 2000 presidential election? It is the uncertainty that makes the result more exciting. Before the days of television great crowds gathered at town halls to hear the returning officer declare the result. This country went to the polls in 1924, just a year after the previous general election. The Tories and the Liberals were the major forces, but their coalition ran into trouble. When the 1923 election results came in, although the Tories had most seats, the improved showing of Labour encouraged the King to invite Ramsay MacDonald to become that party's first prime minister. A minority government is always likely to be unstable. It came as no surprise when another election was called. On 29 October 1924 Guildford waited for its result. There was little doubt about this constituency's result. Staunchly Tory, it recorded the following result: Buckingham (C) 18,273, Markham (Lab) 6,227, Parnell-Kerr (L) 1,924. The shock was in the national vote. The Tories swept back to power with a huge majority.

Above right: It is unlikely that global warming was the topic of conversation for this pair on 23 January 1925. You would have thought that she could at least have passed her brolly down to the poor chap who was up to his knees in floodwater by the Town Bridge. Whatever they were talking about would have been connected with that scourge of this area, overflow from the River Wey. Present day government and environment agencies seem obsessed with shrinking polar ice caps, holes in the ozone layer and carbon dioxide in the atmosphere. Three quarters of a century ago it was simple. It rained, the river overflowed and people got wet. The greenhouse effect was limited to growing tomatoes. Guildford folk saw this sort of spectacle regularly in the last century. There was the flood in 1900 that wrecked the bridge. The couple in the photograph would well recall the great flood of 1906 when tremendous thunderstorms lashed the town. Lightning lit up the sky and the streets turned into torrents. There were to be other problem times not too far round the corner for them to discuss. Around New Year 1928 heavy snowfalls from the previous week melted as there was a sudden rise in temperature. That coincided with a heavy downpour and Guildford was awash once more. The Wey broke its banks in 1936, there were more problems in 1947 and on several occasions in the 1950s. In 1968 High Street was under six feet of water and 300 people were evacuated from their homes. Then the country discovered phrases like 'fossil fuel crisis' and 'trace gases'.

Below: Now, how do you fancy a game of craps? Can I throw snake eyes or hit lucky seven? Perhaps a six will help get me off the mark at Ludo. Maybe I can manage to get on the ladder and climb up the board. All of these thoughts have something to do with dice throwing, but nothing to do with this photograph. The women in earnest concentration at the result of the throw are not in some form of long lost Guildford casino. They are taking part in the ceremony of Maids' Money. This event took place on 22 January 1925 and is a custom that has its roots in the late 17th century. John Howe, in 1674, and John Parsons, in 1702, set up charities that gave rise to the practice. It still takes place annually as part of the work of Guildford Municipal Charities. Held in the Guildhall, it was a prize given to a lucky spinster who was a domestic servant or serving maid. It was worth a tidy little sum when it was first instituted. At the time of this photograph there was still a large number of women employed as cooks, housekeepers and maids in Guildford's many grand houses. In modern times it became difficult to encourage women to apply for the opportunity to roll the dice. After all, there were not many tweenies or scullery maids around. The event was eventually opened up to single women employed in private houses or carers for the elderly in an effort to keep the tradition alive.

Bottom: The golden trefoil of the Girl Guide movement got its first airing in May 1910. Agnes, sister of Robert Baden-Powell, had been encouraged by her brother's ideas that had led to the formation of the Boy Scout movement in July 1907. With the encouragement of Robert she responded to requests from countless girls and young women and formed the association that was to spread across the world. Youth culture is not so new after all. It was also a symbol of the desire for recognition that women sought in the early 20th century. For too long they had been second class citizens. Denied the simplest

of equalities, the right to vote, they showed an interest in and a determination to enjoy traditional male pursuits. The Guides dedicated themselves to good conduct, citizenship training and outdoor activities, just like their male counterparts in the Scouts. However, it was the horror of war that crystallised the place of women in 20th century society. In 1914, when the factory floors were left empty and the fields lay bare of workers, women stepped into the breach. They did not surrender their newly earned status. After the war they demanded official equality with a new fervour. The Guides showed their determination. Here, on 27 June 1925, they took part in a march past at Stoke Park in honour of the Princess Royal's visit to Guildford. They strode behind their banners as proudly as any male battalion and saluted with equal crispness.

In Guildford we have always been proud of our love of the royal family. Visits from any of its representatives brought the crowds onto the streets, whatever the occasion. When the couple on horseback entered the High Street on 27 June 1925 the waiting throngs could hardly control their excitement. They spilled forward over the edge of the kerb to squint down the road towards Quarry Street. Sure enough, there were the cars bringing the royal visitor and her entourage. The limousines had a faintly bucket styled rear end, reminiscent of horse drawn coaches. As they slowly made their way up the hill past Holden's grocery store the cheering began. The object of our affection at that time was Princess Mary. She was the Princess Royal, a title later bestowed on Princess Anne, daughter of our present Queen and Mary's great-niece. Princess Mary married Viscount Lascelles, Earl of Harewood, in February 1922. Their home was the delightful Harewood House in Cottingley, near Bingley in Yorkshire. She was a popular figure in the royal household. As the only daughter of George V's six children she had a special place in his affection and in the hearts of the nation. The reception she received from Guildford residents was matched wherever she went. Born in 1897 she continued in public life right up to her death in 1965.

Above: Every notable point on a timeline is marked with the planting of a tree. The Silver Jubilee of George V was no exception. The Mayor of Guildford, W Sheppard, turned the ceremonial sod as others in the entourage held the infant oak tree steady. The spade was being wielded in Stoke Park. A grand 18th century mansion was once the centrepiece of the park. Built by William Aldersley, it included the 4th Earl of Onslow amongst its owners. It was being used as a school by the time Mayor Sheppard planted his tree. After the war it became part of the technical college. There was a lot of fuss when it was demolished in 1977 as this was another example of the loss of fine architecture. To save it from being developed as building land the 186 acre Stoke Park was bought by the council and opened to the public in 1925. It soon became very popular with families for an afternoon out. Children whizzed around on roller skates and picnics were eaten on the lawns. Toddlers splashed around in the paddling pool and dad loved showing off his prowess on the boating lake with its attractive little bridge across to the island in the middle. Stoke Park was soon established as the venue for the County Show, bringing thousands of visitors from more remote parts of Surrey to enjoy the attractions of the animal classes, crafts, displays and show jumping competitions.

Below centre: These jolly Frenchmen were passing through Guildford on 3 June 1927. In years to come they would be snapped up to play for Arsenal, but these matelots had other ideas. They had shore leave from their ship in Portsmouth harbour. They were on their way to London to enjoy the nightlife in the big city. It would be in the wee small hours when they made their way back to their hammocks to sleep off whatever excesses they had enjoyed. No doubt they were a few francs lighter for the experience. A century before the town had seen Portsmouth to London traffic passing through on a regular basis. That was in the days when horses pulled coaches along the High Street, before the coming of the railway changed the face of travel. By this time charabancs and motor cars travelled the same route in greater comfort and at quicker speeds. All the nice girls love a sailor and a few naughty ones as well. Local girls smiled hopefully in the direction of these Gallic swains, but they were more intent on getting to their destination in the French version of a boys' outing. The men at the kerbside waving them through were happy to see them continue on their way. Surrey men did not have the same je ne sais quoi when it came to charming a girl. There was that something special about the way the French treated their women that set them apart from the British. The local lads were glad they did not stay around to make their entente too cordiale!

The setts in High Street were laid in 1868. The council had to borrow money to meet the £11,000 cost. Henry Peak, who became Guildford's first borough surveyor in 1864, supervised the work. He was also responsible for the building of many of the town's fine Victorian structures. Thanks to him, the Castle Keep was retained. In 1888 it had been under threat of demolition. Another famous son of Guildford made his last journey over the granite setts on Monday, 9 May 1927. Alderman James Baker, Jimmy to everyone who knew him, was held in such high esteem that his funeral cortege brought the crowds onto the streets. A former ploughboy and dairyman, he had risen in status to become mayor in 1907. His humble upbringing meant that he could relate to all classes of society. He represented Holy Trinity ward on the council for 26 years. Jimmy was a hard worker for the community and served on countless committees. He had been a director of the old Borough Halls. He was a prime mover in its conversion into the Theatre Royal in 1912, a project of which he was rightly proud. One of his last wishes was that the theatre should not close during the week that he was laid to rest. He wanted things to continue without any fuss. His sudden death, after complications from a face infection, shocked the town. Holy Trinity Church was packed for his funeral service as people said goodbye to its foremost citizen.

Bottom: It might have come as a shock to even the most knowledgeable of these members of the local division of St John Ambulance Brigade to discover that their roots were in the 11th century. It was a time of the religious crusades to the Holy Land. Disease was more likely to be a killer than any Saracen's scimitar. It was in 1099 that the Knights Hospitaliers of St John set up a military hospital in Palestine. It could cater for over 2,000 patients. It was from the era of Richard the Lionheart that the corps developed. No soccer match or large concert would be complete nowadays without the dark uniforms and white sashes of the St John Ambulance team being present. On hand to lend first aid and help at the first sign of a broken limb on the field or a case of hysteria in the audience, these well trained folk could also be found at village fetes and summer shows. Tending to a touch of sun was well within their brief. Other important work awaited these ranks of smartly turned out volunteers c1926. When the second world war came they more than did their bit. This and other brigades were a branch of the civil defence. They swept into action when our cities were blitzed. There were casualties to be tended and relatives to be comforted. Those were dangerous times and the members responded magnificently, with little thought for their own safety. Tin hats and gas masks became a necessary part of the uniform.

Right: There was once a time you could see boys' knees, made scabby from falling over in the playground. Special seasons were reserved for games of conkers and marbles. For a change, this group had the classroom in mind and not playtime. A bench had been dragged out of the canteen so the lads could have their moment of glory placed on record. They had not won some shield or cup for sporting prowess. Their achievement would have greater significance on their lives. It was the end of the summer term in July 1925. Sandford School was celebrating the brain power these young scholars had displayed in their exams. They had won scholarships to take them to grammar schools. There they would receive specialist academic teaching to prepare them for matriculation and eventual entry to university. A world of Virgil's 'Aeneid' and Homer's 'Iliad' awaited their coming. Then there were the mysteries of the science lab with its Bunsen burners and test tubes. The theories of Pythagoras were ready to be unravelled. All this would be explained by a succession of men in mortar boards and flowing black gowns. School was a place of work. Expectations were high. Everything that was written down had to be produced in perfectly formed copperplate writing, scratched out by a fountain pen or one dipped in an inkwell on the desk. Some schools taught an italic script. Later, the Marian Richardson style became popular. In any case the emphasis was on neatness.

Above: Today's local and county headquarters of St John Ambulance are based at Stocton Close, though in separate buildings. Previously, the Guildford branch was on Leas Road, off Woodbridge Road. A large crowd gathered in the early 1920s to witness the opening ceremony. This building was in use until the late 1960s. It was demolished to make way for the redevelopments taking place around the cattle market. Members of the British Order of St John set up St John Ambulance Brigade in 1887. The idea was to train ordinary people in first aid techniques. Conditions in the workplace were often hazardous. Tired out by long hours of working and endangered by hazardous machinery, there were frequent victims of industrial accidents. St John Ambulance provided emergency medical care in an organised way. The uniformed members soon extended their scope to public events. The Royal Family has always shown a keen interest in the British Order of St John. In 1888 Queen Victoria made it a Royal Order of Chivalry and became its Sovereign Head. In modern times, when Queen Elizabeth, the Queen Mother, celebrated her 100th birthday in 2000 she did so as the Commandant in Chief of St John Ambulance. Her daughter, of course, is now the Sovereign Head. Our Queen's cousin, the Duke of Gloucester, is the Grand Prior of the Order. Today, the Brigade's vehicles assist Surrey's NHS ambulances at weekends.

Top: Before the NHS was born there were fewer doctors and hospital beds than there are today. Nurses of the St John Ambulance Brigade looked after the sick and injured in their own homes. They were kept particularly busy during the latter part of World War I and in the immediate years that followed. There were so many casualties of the war who needed tending. Some of these nurses, pictured c1924, had served as ambulance crew during the conflict. They wore their medals with pride. When hostilities broke out again in 1939 St John and the Red Cross worked together on the home front and overseas. They organised training against gas attacks, ran first aid posts, provided medical reserves and served as volunteer nurses with the forces. St John workers were at the front during the Gulf War in 1991. Women and men are trained to the same high level. The Guildford unit today is a first aid and front line division. It does not just provide carers as some divisions do. The ambulances are all well equipped. They carry similar hardware to that of the NHS ambulances. A St John vehicle will have oxygen, suction units, backboards, head restraints etc. The sole difference is that drugs are not carried. When the familiar black and white uniforms leap into action you know you are in safe hands. St John Ambulance has 47,000 volunteer members, treating 200,000 casualties each year.

The 1935 Silver Jubilee celebrations included carnivals and processions. In this photograph Guildford Fire Brigade was moving along Stoke Road. Drums beat out a rhythm as cornets, trumpets and trombones announced the procession's movement through the lines of people who turned out to enjoy the day. The local fire service was well served by the local company, Dennis Brothers. John Dennis, an ironmonger from Bideford, Devon came to Guildford in 1894. He set up a business with his brother Raymond making and selling bicycles. In 1901 they had expanded sufficiently to own the first purpose built automobile factory in the country. Situated on the corner of Onslow Street and Bridge Street, the company concentrated on producing buses, lorries and fire engines. The first Dennis fire appliances had 45 horsepower engines that powered both the engine and the pump. This did away with the 'steamers' that the fire service used to rely on. They needed a crew to maintain steam pressure as well as one to fight the fire. The earliest appliances to roll out of the 1872 fire station on North Street were horse drawn. Boys were employed to run down the street shouting or ringing a bell to get the volunteer fire crew out of their homes. Response times were so slow that the fire service was often too late in arriving to be very effective. But the motorised brigades and their officers, who eventually became full time, were able to react to situations in time to save many businesses and houses from complete devastation. The old fire station is now both a public toilet and a listed building!

Below: The procession along the bypass in 1935 seemed to snake along forever. Marching bands led the way. Every club, business and society imaginable seemed to be represented. It was remarkable that anyone was left to stand on the verges and roadside to wave and cheer as the floats and tableaux went by. The road was constructed during 1933, cutting a great swathe across Stoke Park. The official opening ceremony took place in 1935. The need for such a bypass had been apparent for years. The huge increase in car ownership led to old market towns, like Guildford, grinding to a halt under the weight of traffic. Roads designed for horse drawn vehicles could not cope with the influx of motor vehicles that came along between the wars. The bypass was a fast highway that brought its own problems. Through traffic was kept from the town centre, but the road became a dangerous racetrack. As greater volumes of traffic flew along the carriageway, the number of accidents increased. Perhaps the most famous one to hit the headlines was on 22 January 1959. Mike Hawthorn, a former Dennis Brothers' apprentice, had become the first Briton to win the world motor racing championship. This popular, debonair driver was killed when he crashed his 3.4 litre Jaguar on the bypass. By then, the benefits of the new road had been lost to the town centre. The 'never had it so good' era had seen car ownership rocket again and Guildford was once more grinding to a halt.

Bottom: Pictured c1941 Pewley Fort Home Guard was one of countless groups of volunteers who were ready to repel the enemy should the invasion ever come. At that time it was still a real threat. Although by the autumn of 1940 Hitler had abandoned Operation Sea Lion, his plan to invade Britain, his forces could still have been mobilised. We had won the aerial Battle of Britain and earned some breathing space. But, the Luftwaffe might have turned its attention from blitzing our cities to dicing with the RAF once more. Fortunately for us and the future pattern of the war Hitler went east. His divisions attacked Russia in the summer of 1941. If he had revived Operation Sea Lion he would have been faced with a collection of World War I veterans, youngsters and men unfit for the forces or in reserved occupations. The Pewley force contained such a mixture. Some look to be well into their 60s. One lad near the middle of the second row could only have been about 16. Another at the left end of the back row was similarly youthful. It is doubtful that they possessed the weaponry or physical fitness that would have enabled them to beat off a Panzer division. What was not in doubt was their commitment and bravery. They would have given their all to defend home and family from the enemy.

personnel fighting overseas. The rest of the television series did not do them justice. The Home Guard was not the bumbling outfit it was portrayed to be. Admittedly, when initially formed as the Local Defence Volunteers, some of early efforts were ridiculous. One platoon patrolled with imitation rifles once used in a Drury Lane production. Elsewhere catapults were recommended as launching pads for petrol bombs and broomsticks were converted into pikes when knives were attached. The force was renamed the Home Guard in July 1940 and 250,000 men were enrolled. Although still handicapped by a shortage of weapons and resources, they trained with vigour and initiative. Cornhill Insurance Company had its own unit, the Shalford House Home Guard. The chap in civvies was the general manager, Claude Wilson. Others in the line up included Ernie Hide, Doug Willis, Monty Morant, Bert Freeman, Stan Harper, Wally Lambert, Stan George, Ray Wass, John Turner and Bob Reynolds. If a Nazi paratrooper landed and tried to pass himself off as a loss adjuster these fellows would twig him straight away.

Right: The popular BBC TV sitcom 'Dad's Army' made audiences laugh in the 1970s and 1980s. Repeats in later years were no less successful. The country's living rooms rocked to viewers' merriment at the antics of a Home Guard unit run by a pompous bank manager. Its members included old soldiers, an undertaker, a butcher and a trainee bank clerk. That much was accurate. They were just the sort of people that volunteered to join a force entrusted with guarding key installations and sworn to protect those left at home by service

'God save the Queen' was what it said on the proclamation paper. No one had needed to make that rousing call for over half a century. The Lord Lieutenant of Surrey stood outside Holy Trinity Church to give the message to the crowd assembled at the top of High street. In the background a bus turned towards North Street. Those listening to the announcement had mixed feelings. They had heard of the death of King George VI with sadness. He had been with them during the dark hours of the second world war. He had not slipped away to some quiet corner of the Commonwealth. The Royal Family stayed in this country and took its chance like the rest of us. Even Buckingham Palace fell victim to the Blitz. That was when his consort, Queen Elizabeth, said that she could now look London's eastenders in the face. The King had steadied the country following the abdication crisis created by his brother's affair with the American socialite, Wallis Simpson. Now, on 6 February 1952, the King was dead at the tender age of 56. The Lord Lieutenant proclaimed a new monarch, Queen Elizabeth II. She was only 25. The church had been the centre point for many important announcements during its long history. James Horne built it in the middle of the 18th century. Holy Trinity is Surrey's only large Georgian church and contains the tomb of George Abbot, a former Archbishop of Canterbury. The hospital he endowed is on the opposite side of High Street. Like the church, it is also a grade I listed building.

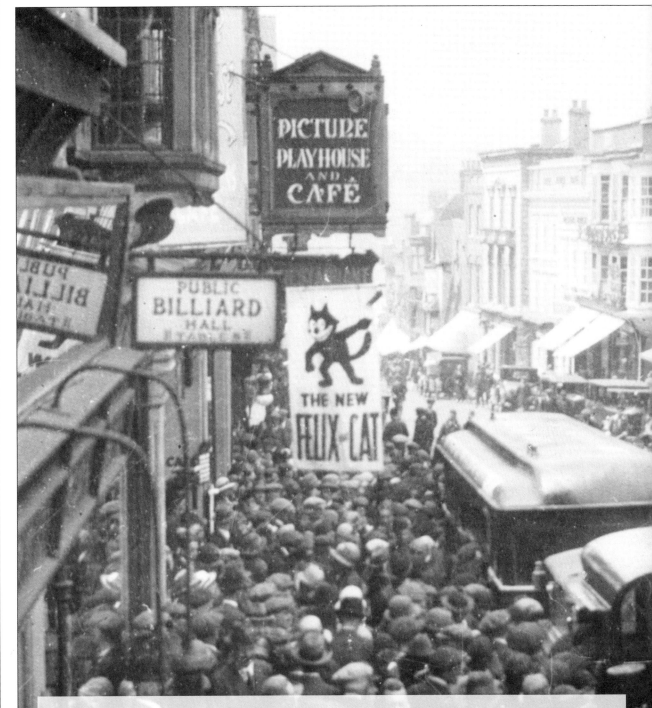

The Picture Playhouse opened in 1922, becoming part of County Cinemas in 1929. Odeon Theatres took a controlling interest in later years. It closed on 12 June 1965 with a double bill of Norman Wisdom films, 'The Bulldog Breed' and 'The Square Peg'. Demolished in 1966, the site was replaced by a supermarket. However, it was neither the cinema nor its café that attracted large crowds onto High Street in 1926. The multitude had started to gather at about 11.30 in the morning. By 12.30 it had swollen to several hundreds. Energetic ringing of a bell mounted on its Yankee boiler announced the arrival of a marvel of modern engineering, the trackless train. The sight of the petrol engined machine impressed cheering onlookers. The observation style saloon coach was sumptuously fitted out. The train had travelled 23,000 across Europe and America. In Guildford it was being used as an advertising medium for the British Legion. The Playhouse manager, Mr R Eggleton, and Mr M Driscoll, the secretary of the local branch of the British Legion, had arranged its coming to the High Street. The train spent the rest of the day parked on North Street before moving on to Oxford. If anyone ever laughs at you for saying that trains used to run along High Street, just ask them to put his money where his mouth is. Then show him this picture and collect your cash.

On the move

Above: This is a sight to gladden the heart of any anorak. Show the photograph to any trainspotter and his eyes will glaze over. A sight such as this is the reason behind all those notebooks full of numbers. Little lads who hung over railway bridges, jotting away on scruffy bits of paper, have grown into an army of people keen to preserve this form of transport. They want the modern generation to understand the power and majesty of the steam locomotive. The 5MT, 700 S15 engine was being coaled up in the mainline station. It was just one in a long line of locos that brought new settlers to the town in the second half of the 19th century. Many set up home in the villas along Stoke Road and the other streets that ringed the town.

Shopkeepers appeared from the carriages that the engines pulled. They had come to Guildford to replace the many innkeepers who had relied on the passing trade brought by coach travel. By late Victorian times Guildford was a place to call home rather than pass through. The mainline station linked the south coast with the capital. Via its suburban line through London Road station, it gave the villages of Clandon, Horsley and Cobham contact with the outside world. The British fascination for steam locomotives was best shown in the interest generated whenever a speed record was broken. The Flying Scotsman, Silver Jubilee, Coronation Scot and Mallard were all front page news between 1934 and 1938 as the record was raised from 97 to 126 mph.

Above: The coming of the electric train to Guildford was such an important event that there was a special ceremonial opening to mark the occasion. It was heralded by an official procession along High Street, led by the mayor, the stationmaster, the town crier and dignitaries and officials from the town council and railway company. Residents were so interested in the way their world was changing so rapidly that they lined the streets all the way down to the station. There was no pushing and shoving. People were orderly in 1925. It only needed one bobby as a token form of crowd control. No ropes, no barriers and no lines of police linking arms. They were not needed. The British public was more restrained in those days. Guildford could boast two railway stations. As a central point in the district it displayed the confidence that the railway age had in itself by having two lines entering the town. The main line station served as a stopping point for long distance traffic. The station at London Road served the suburban line that took commuters from Guildford and the outlying villages into the capital. The two lines divided at Surbiton to allow the secondary route to meander through the Surrey countryside. Railways were intended to give greater access to the rest of the country for us all. They also provided generations of small boys with the hobby of trainspotting that many continued into adulthood. Electrification of the trains did not replace the love that so many people felt for the age of steam. Even today there is something truly exciting about the sight of a plume of smoke from an old locomotive funnel or the sound of its whistle. Cleaner travel does not have the same sense of history or mystery.

Above right: 'Oyez, oyez, oyez.' The ancient role of the town crier was being played out in the summer of July 1925. Dressed in his ceremonial robes he was reading the proclamation that announced the coming of the electric train service to the London to Guildford line. Local dignitaries donned their top hats in honour of the occasion. Children clustered to the front of the crowd to catch a glimpse of a tradition that amused them. These youngsters were part of a generation growing up on a diet of BBC radio that brought them the news. Their parents appreciated the historic significance of the way in which important events were relayed. They, of course, had newspapers, but they were only too well aware that for centuries beforehand the town crier had been the source of news for the common man. Train travel had helped Guildford become an important commuter town. The London and South West Railway had reached Woking in 1838. Guildford station opened on 5 May 1845 and the direct line to Portsmouth was completed in 1859. In a stroke the town became a central point for commuter land, both to the capital and to the dockyards of the south coast. Electrification of the London line meant even smoother travel. It was a sign of the dawning of yet another age of modern travel in a century that had already seen huge developments on road and in the air.

The electrification of the new Guildford line to London was marked by special celebrations on 9 July 1925. Schoolchildren turned up in their numbers to welcome this modern development that for nearly a century had relied on steam power. Men waved their hats as the guard waved his flag to get the first new loco rolling along the track. Electrification of the main line followed in 1937. With it came a growth in population that added to the town's reputation as being home to people who were 'something in the city'. After the second world war trains were full of men in business suits wearing bowler hats. With furled umbrellas tucked under their arms they took their places in the carriages with military precision. Out came the Times crossword. On the journey to Waterloo pencils flew across the cryptic clues and filled in the squares with a religious intensity. Men would make that journey day in and day out for years. Quite often they sat in the same seat and next to the same identically dressed businessman for each journey. They seldom exchanged pleasantries. It was not the done thing to engage in idle chitchat with a complete stranger. The British reserve meant that you minded your own business. In the evening the wives crowded the car park as they waited to collect their husbands and take them home for the evening meal. 'Good day at the office, dear?' 'Yes, thank you, dear.' Then it was a sherry before dinner, an early night and off to start the round all over again.

Bottom: In the early years of the 20th century if you were going to wear a cap, make sure it was a big one. That was the fashion statement being made by this chap standing alongside this bus. It was one of the fleet owned by Guildford and District Motor Services Ltd. It ran from the town to Walton-on-Thames, calling at Woking, Chertsey and Weybridge on the way. The women wore high necked blouses decorated with costume jewellery, topped off with large hats that restricted the view of anyone sitting behind them. This style of clothing was swept away by the innovative Coco Chanel in the 1920s. Her original use of jersey fabric to create a 'poor girl' look attracted the attention of influential wealthy women seeking relief from the prevalent corseted styles. Hairstyles became more boyish and little cloche hats came to replace the wide brims and high crowns as Chanel influenced style between the wars. The men at the back of the bus were sporting jolly boaters and blazers. Perhaps they were off for a day's punting along the river. Guildford and District was one of a number of companies that plied their trade around the town at this time. Together with some of the smaller companies, it was swallowed up by Aldershot and District Traction Company c1920. This Guildford bus was photographed outside the old Congregational Church on High Street. The former Theatre Royal is in the background.

Right: This open topped charabanc belonged to Norman's of Ridgemount and was a former Safeguard coach. In the first half of the last century all coaches, whatever their style, were nicknamed 'charas'. The true charabanc was a car with bench seats, the literal translation from French, but the name was applied generally to all coaches on pleasure trips. The first bus services developed after the demise of the stagecoach. In the first half of the

19th century 15 stagecoaches passed through Guildford on a daily basis. After the coming of the railway, by 1851 this number had fallen to just three. Something was needed to bridge the gap between the long distance stagecoach and the railway for the areas not served by train. On 17 April 1883 West Metropolitan Tramways Company launched Surrey's first horse drawn tram service. With the help of Dennis Brothers' motor buses the early 1900s saw the formation of many small private companies operating routes in and around Guildford. After World War I day trips to the seaside became popular. Family groups, societies, church organisations and workmates hired 'charas' or booked seats on them. Off they went to Southsea, Bognor Regis, Littlehampton, Worthing and Brighton. The group in this photograph would have to hang on to their hats as they bowled along the road to the coast. It did not worry too much about the conditions. It was off on an adventure that, in a few short years, would become commonplace. Epsom Coaches, Surrey Motors, Cooke's Coaches and Pearl Grey all offered similar services for those in search of sea and sand.

June 1927 it was in collision with a car. The bus overturned, badly injuring a Clandon woman who required hospital treatment. Sightseers gathered to view the scene as council workmen righted the bus and waited for the breakdown truck. Safety features, such as Percy Shaw's cats' eyes and the Belisha beacon, belonged to the next decade. In the meantime, Epsom Road had added another statistic to the list.

Top: Farnham Road bus station was in full swing as the town got back to normality after World War II. Although Guildford showed little obvious signs of the war, suffering only minor damage from occasional bombing raids, there were still the after effects shared by the

Above: Today's roads are dangerous with cars whizzing along them at high speed. We have motorway pile-ups, road rage and concertina crashes galore. However, it was no better in the early days of motoring. Despite the smaller numbers of vehicles and the lower speeds they could reach, our roads were death traps. The statistics made frightening reading. Most rural roads after the first world war were little improvement on those that had been used by horse and cart in earlier times. At best they would be simple strips of tarmac, with a stone base. Few had any form of lighting and there was no proper form of regulation for drivers. The compulsory driving test was not introduced until the 1930s. Yet, by 1926 there were 1.75 million motor vehicles on the road. The death toll, particularly amongst pedestrians, was high. In 1927 experimental signs were put up in London to remind them to look right or left, as appropriate, when crossing a one way street. Roads began to have white markings painted on them to denote carriageways. None of this was of much use to the driver of the vehicle from the Rural Bus Company. On 24

rest of the country. Fireside chairs lay empty. RAF aircrew, Royal Navy personnel or members of the Queen's Regiment battalions who failed to make that final journey home would never again fill them. Rationing bit hard. Food and clothing was in short supply. Petrol supplies were low, so people turned to public transport for those essential journeys. In the 1920s there were still some open topped buses in operation. Passengers on the top deck were warned to be wary of railway bridges, overhanging trees and telegraph wires. Standing upstairs was not to be recommended! Bus travel had expanded in between the wars. In 1926 Charles Dobbs ran an hourly Skylark service to Oxford Circus. By 1930 London General was running its Green Line network that included the G route from Guildford to London. The London Passenger Transport Board came into effect in 1933. When these pictured passengers streamed away from the bus station across the bridge into High Street they were glad of the service. Their cars remained in their garages until petrol supplies eased. Then our traffic problems really began.

Shopping spree

Above: This used to be known as Ram Corner. It took its name from the Ram Inn that stood to the left of the photograph until 1913. The old pub stuck out into the road, making it very difficult for traffic to negotiate the corner. Even in those far off days it had become known as one of Surrey's worst traffic black spots. When the Ram and several other adjacent buildings were demolished the flow improved a little, but modern day road users will know this part of Guildford as still being an awkward place in which to manoeuvre. It is where Chertsey Street combines with North Street near the junction with High Street. Traffic lights now control this T junction and traffic

coming from the right, along the upper High Street, can no longer continue straight across, but must turn down the hill. Access to the lower High Street is not allowed. Massey's chemist shop, on the corner, is now Ryman's stationery shop. In October 1925 you could get a cup of tea at the Excelsior café at no 8, to the right of the photograph. Mr and Mrs AE Harrison had just left 9 and 9A, next left, for a house in Worthing and had been bought out by EH Rhodes. Biddle's well known stationer's was at no 10, down the passage. The opening to the left of the corner block, as we view it, is Pannell's Court. It provides a cut through to the Grammar School and Allen House Gardens.

You could hardly miss noticing that this was Timothy White's. We criticise present day society for its bold and brash advertising. Perhaps we have forgotten that discreet shop signs were not universal in the late 1920s either. Rival store, Boot's, had a similar shop front. Perhaps it was something peculiar to chemists that they had to shout rather than whisper their existence. The shops pictured were strangely numbered. The chemist was 39 High street and HC King's Guildford Meat Stores was 39 1/2. The Red Lion once stood on this corner with Market Street. It dated from the 16th century, but did not become important until the 1600s. The hotel boasted 50 beds and included the diarist Samuel Pepys, who was then clerk to the Admiralty, amongst its visitors. He would have been on his way to the dockyards at Portsmouth. In 1660 King Charles II spent a night at the Red Lion. He was in Guildford to receive a town plate to mark the Restoration. Another famous town landmark stood across the other side of Market Street. The Bull's Head was a hostelry dating from about the same time as the Red Lion. Sadly, it ceased to exist as a pub towards the end of the 20th century after years of controversy about its change if use. Where the Red Lion and Timothy White's once stood the 21st century shopper can now visit River Island.

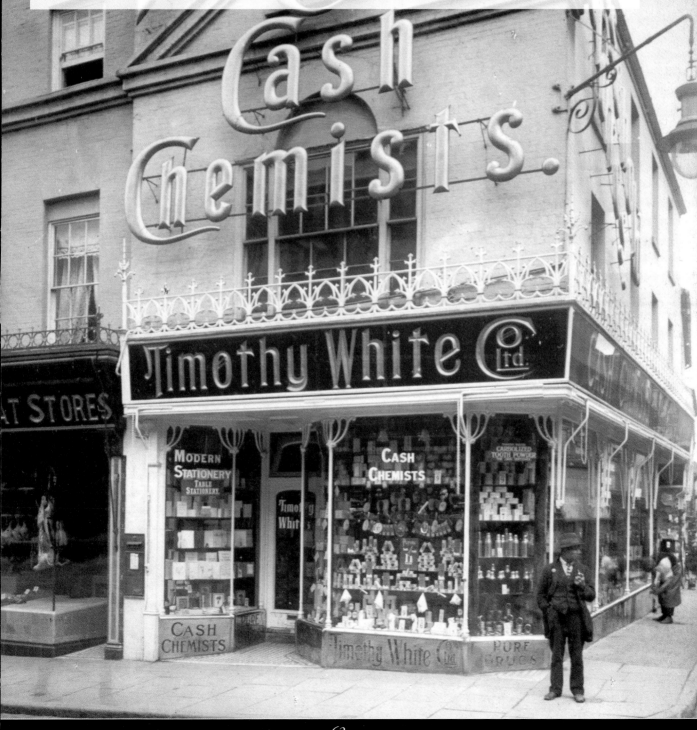

The beautifully gilded clock on the Guildhall is one of the most prominent sites in the town. Here it was lit by floodlight as part of the 1935 Silver Jubilee celebrations. The hall stands where an even older one could be found in medieval times. The present building dates from Tudor times and is a grade I listed building. Thanks to public subscription, the facade was added in 1683, when the clock case was also first seen. Its mechanism was much older, going back to early Elizabethan times. In the 19th century the old dial was replaced by a glass one lit by gas, but the original parts were restored in 1898. The first bell came from St Martha's, the church on top of the Chilworth ridge to which so many locals have taken an after Sunday lunch walk over the years. The Guildhall's iron balcony has been used for countless proclamations, from announcements of royal births to declarations of war. The 16th century courtroom has a set of standard measures that were donated to Guildford by Elizabeth I. There are few others like it in existence. The Guildhall houses a number of the borough treasures. It is the venue of the mayor making ceremony each May. The Guildhall and its protruding clock have long been one of the town's most significant landmarks. Many a couple has arranged to meet there before going off together for a Saturday night out.

Below: The photographer stood alongside St Nicolas' Church on 11 December 1960. There has been a church there since medieval times. This church, consecrated on 20 April 1876, replaced one only built in 1836. Its attractive tower was built to a design by SS Teulon. He retained portions of the 15th century structure. It is a grade II listed, three stage edifice, topped by a bell chamber. Close to the river, this area often floods. There are markings on the walls that indicate various water levels over the years. Bury Street separates St Nicolas from the building that was occupied by the caterer F Ayres and Sons and an estate agent, E Gascoigne-Pees. It is now a set of offices called Mauritius House. It stands at the end of lower High Street, where it meets the A3100 to Portsmouth. Across this road, heading up the hill past the 'No through road' sign, finds you on The Mount. The building on the corner, next to the overhead street lamp, was the Weyside Temperance Hotel. It had once been the Weyside Coffee Tavern. The hotel was demolished in the early 1960s and replaced with two blocks of flats. Travel about a mile along the Mount and you come to another listed building. Henley Fort was built in 1896 as one of 13 similar defences against possible invasion by the French. It is ironic that 18 years later we would be marching off to war in their defence.

Bottom: Pause at this spot on Market Street today and you will be looking at Jones' Bootmakers and Neal's Yard Remedies. Now take a trip back in time when fish, poultry and game was on display. The smell of freshly caught salmon washed across the pavement to tempt shoppers coming to the long established Phillips' establishment. Scottish salmon was a delicacy brought down from the river Tay to tickle the palates of gourmands at the bargain price of half a crown a pound for a middle cut. That is 12.5p in today's money. The tail end was 3d (1p) cheaper. The shop assistants sold ice in small or large quantities to keep the fish fresh for the journey home. Wall's sausages would provide a hearty breakfast. They had a real tangy taste to them, unlike the bland supermarket chipolata we have now. You can imagine them sizzling and spitting in the pan, ready to topped off with a plateful of scrambled farmyard eggs. If salmon was not your choice, then what about duck a l'orange? An English bird for 1s 8d (8p) per lb would make a sumptuous dinner. The Phillips shop stacked its foodstuffs close to the roadside so that the housewife could not help herself from stopping. There was little chance that she could turn down the opportunity to take home such fine food. In warm weather the poultry and game was put into the cold room at the back. Sometimes you could have the wrong sort of aroma!

'Let Burton dress you' said the slogan on the shop front. 'The tailor of taste' was also home to a snooker and billiards hall in its upstairs rooms. Young men ignored the advice of their mothers that such establishments were places for misspent youth. When you are young what else do you want to do with your youth than spend it unwisely? There is time enough to act like a responsible citizen in later life. Many of the snooker halls were temperance establishments, so no evil drink was on sale. However, they were often places where large bets were struck and bookies' runners operated on behalf of their paymasters. The snooker table was a good place to hustle a living. A gullible player would be challenged to a game for a small stake. When he won easily the bet was increased tenfold. The hustler suddenly started playing with side, screw and stun like Joe Davis at his best. A fool and his money were soon parted. The hustler could now afford to get 'the full Monty', a complete set of clothes from Montague Burton. The expression came into our language thanks to men returning from the armed forces and buying demob clothing. Burton's shops were on every main street from Exeter to Newcastle, as a sign in the window proclaimed. This High Street store is now occupied by Gap. But, if you look closely today, the name of Burton is still in the same place at the top of the building.

Making a living

The collapsed sign says 'Road closed for repairs'. It hardly matters. The debris and clutter made it fairly obvious to anyone approaching Market Street that resurfacing and concreting was well under way. The work began on 16 February 1934. The road was closed for a week before traffic was allowed to return. but the shops continued to trade. Heading up towards High Street, along the right hand side of Market Street, there were Lavell's, Lipton Ltd and an establishment selling rugs, mats and bedding, where the Imperial Commercial Hotel once traded. Home Colonial was further along. These days you will find French Connection at 67 North Street, on the left corner. The council workmen, in their mufflers and flat caps, were busy with their wheelbarrows and concrete mixers on this crisp winter's day. Edward Elgar, perhaps England's finest composer since Purcell, died as they came to the end of their repair work. It is unlikely that they whistled his 'Pomp and Circumstance' marches as they toiled away. 'Smoke gets in your eyes' or 'Stormy weather' would have been more to their liking. These had nothing to do with the Woodbines dangling from their lips or the rain that fell. They were the top pop tunes of the day. Workmen and delivery lads whistled away happily as they got on with their business. Try to do that today with the latest ditty from Puff Daddy or Fat Boy Slim.

There is only one thing more appealing than a smile on the face of a pretty girl. It is smiles on the faces of several of them. These lovely ladies were tucking into lunch in the canteen at Shalford House. They were taking a well earned break from their duties with Cornhill Insurance. Perhaps they were sharing a joke about the wording of an insurance claim. There were always some howlers when the claimant wrote something that could be interpreted in a rude or amusing way. One woman stated that she could not be blamed for crashing the car as she was 'under the doctor' at the time! They might have been tickled by something they heard on 'Workers' Playtime' or some other radio programme. The escapades of Tommy Handley in 'ITMA' or the humour of Elsie and Doris Waters as Gert and Daisy always got a laugh in the 1940s. Let us hope that the girls had not been listening to one of cheeky chappie Max Miller's jokes taken from his blue book. Those were a bit too near the knuckle for this set of charmers. The conversation across the canteen table might have moved on to what they were doing on Saturday night. They could go to the pictures and enjoy a Hollywood melodrama such as 'The Hour before the Dawn' with Franchot Tone and Veronica Lake. Alternatively, they could go dancing to a band playing Glenn Miller's 'In the Mood'. Those winning smiles would soon find dancing partners.

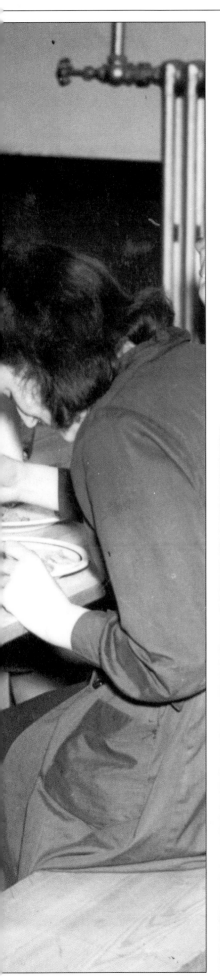

Below: In September 1939 the London offices of Cornhill Insurance only possessed one radio. It was kept in the general manager's office. He opened the window so that the workforce could hear the words of the prime minister. The British government had demanded that Germany should end its invasion of Poland. When Neville Chamberlain said, 'No such undertaking has been received,' the country knew it was at war. Cornhill, in company with many other firms, moved its London base to the suburbs. The city was fearful of aerial bombardment. It had seen what had taken place during the Spanish Civil War. A skeleton staff was left in London, but the bulk of the office files, equipment and personnel moved to Guildford. Cornhill took over Shalford House. As the company knew that the war was to likely to be a long affair it even put up temporary dormitories for its staff. Routine was soon established. Work on the files held in the employers' liability department carried on in the 1940s, just as it had done before the war. Only the site was different. The desks and seats had a basic look about them, but the office manager seems to have ensured that he got a decent chair. In front of him the men all wore business suits and ties. The one using a 'horn' was making an early contribution to automation in speeding up administration. The women wore overalls to carry out their jobs. After the war some staff moved back to London, but Shalford House was used until 1954 when Cornhill relocated to its present Guildford site. The house was demolished later in the decade.

Left: Cornhill Insurance moved offices in 1954. It took over a former tannery near the A3. Soon the typewriters were clacking away and the bells were ringing to remind the typists to bash the little carriage return handle. Compare this office scene with one you might see today. There is not a computer monitor in sight. Even an electric typewriter was a piece of hardware that was still a luxury. Audio typing was the nearest these women got to anything remotely technological. They plugged an earpiece into a tape recording the boss had dictated earlier. Using a foot pedal to control the playback speed, they pounded the keys to produce official letters. Each one had a piece of carbon paper and another sheet of paper underneath so that a copy could be kept. No records on hard disk or state of the art photocopy machines for these women. Their office had them sitting in rows. There were no banks of phones to use. Nor were there any screens to give them a sense of their own personal space. In the morning they got dressed ready for work. Casual attire was for weekends. Jeans were for manual labourers. The cardigan was a common fashion item, as were the strings of pearls that several of them wore. Hair was cut fairly short and neatly permed with just a hint of a Toni wave. At night school some of them learned Pitman shorthand so that they could move out of the typing pool and become secretaries.

Below: The young lad on the front row must have thought that he had just exchanged one desk for another. A short time earlier he had been in school. Now he was in the world of work at Cornhill's motor claims department. New boys were sometimes used as 'gophers'. 'Go for this or go for that,' was the message. Two months previously another lad had been sent out for a packet of 10 Senior Service. He was told that if he could not find any then, 'Get me something else.' He came back with a pork pie. His gopher days were over. There was plenty of other work to be done. The shelves on the walls creaked under the weight of the files and folders stored on them. Shalford House was pressed into service as an emergency base for Cornhill Insurance during World War II. Even though petrol rationing kept many cars in their garages in the 1940s, there were still plenty of claims to be processed. The blackout led to a large number of accidents. Drivers tried to find their way round at night by trusting to a mixture of memory, skill and good luck. Their failures ended up here. Some of the women were wearing a type of uniform. Was this company policy or were they off on civil defence duties after work?

Pressing Business

Before the introduction of printing, books were copied by hand by monks, how they must have yearned for a machine to do the work. Printing is an ancient and honoured craft which can trace its history from China through to the invention of movable metal type in Germany and to its later introduction to England by Thomas Caxton. Since then the printing industry has been subject to countless improvements and innovations.

The second half of the twentieth century saw printing transformed by technical changes, which would have amazed earlier practitioners of the craft. Its limited world was invaded by photography and electronics, and transformed in a new industrial revolution. Biddles, the well-known printers and book binders of Guildford, are used to looking ahead to see developments around the next corner but this story is concerned with Biddles' past and its origins in the high Victorian era. It was then a totally different world - and yet the idea of keeping abreast of new technical developments was there at the start.

The story is that of a family business. The principal characters are Charles A Biddle and his son Leonard. Charles first set up as a printer in Alton, Hampshire; the family moved to Guildford in 1883. After gaining experience in Winchester and Kettering, Leonard Biddle joined his father, and their new business was launched in 1885. A surviving picture with a truly Victorian quality shows Charles and two of his small children outside his shop on the corner of Martyr Road and Haydon Place. The building is

little changed today, though no longer connected with Biddles.

A record of the firm's first days' trading still exists: on 3rd February 1885, fifty small cards were sold, and the following day 100 small business cards, the total gain from these transactions being two shillings and four pence. However modest this appears, they were the early shoots of a harvest that proved unfailing and substantial. Guildford already had numerous printers including names like Russell and Lasham - but the growing town easily found room and work for one more.

The long-established firm of Lasham was later taken over by Biddles and this involved an interesting literary connection with the district. Lashams had printed 'Stephan Langton', an historical romance by Martin Tupper featuring 'The Silent Pool' near Guildford. Biddles continued to publish this popular book, and it was still in print in the 1940s, despite Tupper's name being practically forgotten by then.

Top: Company founder Charles WA Biddle with his wife. ***Above right:*** *A printing plate for a programme issued to mark Guildford's celebrations on the occasion of King George V's coronation in 1911.* ***Right:*** *Charles and two of his children outside the shop on the corner of Martyr Road and Haydon Place in the late 19th century.*

Stationery Office in London, local hospitals and schools in the area such as Guildford Grammar School, Charterhouse and Bedales. Biddles even took over a newspaper, 'The Weekly Free Press' from its original founder and produced it for many years - at first actually free, and later selling for one penny - later still it became the Guildford Times. Another interesting local connection was with the famous spiritual healer, Harry Edwards of Shere: Biddles brought out Edwards' magazine 'The Healer' for a number of years.

However, Biddles were mainly general and jobbing printers. Later the printing of books for publishers became its speciality, remaining so today.

The general work was very varied - and according to some former employees the variety itself was enjoyable. At first every local community has many different needs which keep a printer busy; later he will go further afield to satisfy his voracious printing presses, and Biddles naturally did this. Local activity included humble items like tradesmen's bags, butter wrappers, tea papers, meat-tickets for butchers, billheads, compliment slips, labels, timetables, magazines - all in endless variety.

Over the years, the customers included official bodies such as the Surrey County Council and the

The family business in the little corner shop was a success. A move to new purpose built premises took place in 1888: the address was 22 Haydon Place where various subsequent improvements and extensions would be made.

Above: *Staff on a company outing in 1923.*
Right: *An early delivery vehicle.*
Below: *Staff pictured in the 1920s.*

The staff increased rapidly from a mere handful to about 30 at the time the first world war broke out in 1914. Biddles survived the Great War despite the inevitable loss of staff, the austere conditions, the shortage of paper and other materials. In 1919, one year after the war ended, the firm was incorporated as Biddles Limited.

when an impressive new building was opened in Martyr Road, very close to Biddles' previous location. This outward and visible sign of expansion marked Biddles' importance in the town and surrounding areas. It was a time when advertising and 'public relations' were making great strides, and the next year the firm's first publicity booklet was produced, full of confident yet well founded claims. Within a decade Biddles was being described as one of the largest and most prosperous printing businesses in the South of England as well as one of the most forward thinking - in the 1920s the firm became one of the first in the country to install a Linotype composing machine.

The true 'family firm' has become rare today, but Biddles has always deserved this label in its truest sense. Relations between staff and management were always friendly and cordial with remarkably few disagreements. In 1911 the staff had presented a letter to Leonard Biddle thanking him for reducing working hours. In 1919 the hours were further reduced (to 48 per week) and one week's holiday with pay was introduced. In the following year an artistic member of staff, WD Smith, was asked to hand-letter and illustrate a 'testimonial' to Leonard Biddle expressing the esteem and good feeling which they had for him: 43 members of staff put their names to this, and a sketch of the Haydon Place building was included - a useful piece of documentation of a works which no longer exists. One of the most important dates of the Biddles story was 1923

Staff continued to be well looked after. Biddles had a very good Sports and Social Club. Cricket and other games were played at various locations around the town. There were splendid dances, with music provided by military bands from Aldershot. The Club started in 1923 and its popularity did much to cement the family feeling in the firm over the years.

Top: *A poster from the early 20th century.*
Right: *Biddles shop decorated to celebrate the Queen's coronation in 1953.*

Biddles had always been in the stationery trade and the first separate shop for this had been opened in 1922 at 12, High Street. By 1925 this also proved too small and a move to much larger premises at No. 10 took place. This made possible the addition of other departments: a bookshop a typewriter showroom and a lending library. Subsequently the widening of Guildford's High Street was proposed which necessitated moving once more, and No. 164 became Biddles' third retail premises - although the projected road widening was not completed for many years.

The staff had doubled by 1928 when a group photo was presented to Leonard Biddle accompanied by another skilfully executed booklet by W D Smith, containing 115 signatures.

When the Martyr Road premises were built, the supply of electricity in Guildford was unreliable. The local power station was apt to break down and there were frequent interruptions. To avoid such expensive delays, Biddles' new building had its own power plant. Two large gas engines were installed in a specially constructed engine house at the rear. Gas-producing plant and generators were added and sufficient current produced to light the whole building, drive about 60 machines and work the lift which served all four floors. No town supply at all was used at that time.

In less than twelve years the premises were already becoming cramped, hindering further development. Fortunately there was space available at the rear and in 1935 an extension to every floor was planned plus a fifth storey, nearly doubling the floor space. An additional lift was included, and a sprinkler system was installed throughout the whole building in case of fire.

In 1935 the firm celebrated fifty years of business and Leonard Biddle, described by those who knew him as reserved rather than extrovert, gentle yet decidedly firm when necessary, announced his retirement. Leonard Biddle credited the firm's success to the efforts of his three sons. Others gave Leonard himself the credit: after retirement he lived another ten years, dying in 1945 at the close of the second world war.

Left: *Biddles' first stationery shop at 12 High Street in 1922.* **Below:** *The Martyr Road site incorporating the stationery shop in 1964.*

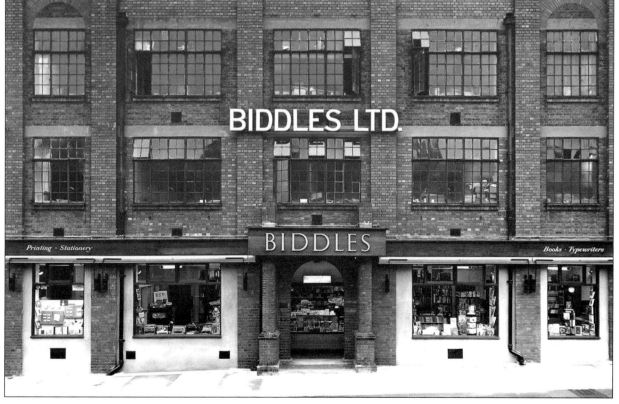

During the second world war half of the Martyr Road factory was commandeered by the Air Ministry and an engineering firm worked there day and night making air-filters for British aircraft. At the war's close staff had to busy themselves with restoring normal conditions, though many would later recall the state of austerity which continued for a considerable time and an industry facing innumerable problems even after serving staff had returned and the works was again devoted to its proper purpose.

On the stationery side of the business there was a major change in 1964 when the shop left its old premises in Guildford's High Street (now owned by Austin Reed), and moved to the printing establishment in Martyr Road, where it occupied the ground floor from then on.

Early in the seventies Biddles began a programme of reorientation and re-equipment. The aim was now to concentrate on publishers' work and acquire new machinery to cope with the latest techniques and processes. By 1974 Biddles had ceased to set type cast in hot metal. This followed the trend of the whole industry, which was soon to abandon metal type almost completely, breaking a tradition as old as the craft of printing itself. The revolution involved what was known as 'cold composition', and the printing process for this was 'offset lithography'.

The conversion being completed, Biddles began to specialise in complex page make-up and book-impositions. In due course the firm's skill was rewarded by prizes and awards within the industry.

Top: *A line-up of company vehicles in 1936.*
Above centre: *Biddles premises in 1936.*
Right: *Late 20th century folding machinery.*

Book production requires a number of operations which are not always undertaken under one roof, but many publishers want the printers to also handle the binding of their publications. Needing to expand its binding operations, in 1977 Biddles

acquired the assets of a bindery in Kings Lynn, Norfolk, which became a wholly-owned subsidiary.

Another important development took place in 1978 when Biddles moved some of its activities to Walnut Tree House, a modern factory and office building in Woodbridge Park near the River Wey. The purpose was to go into book printing by web offset (printing on the 'roll' instead of the single sheet) with its accompanying speed and economy. A new showroom for business machinery was opened at this address.

The founder of the firm would have agreed that a printer must have the latest equipment, but Charles Biddle would have been startled to hear of machinery reaching the Guildford works from far-off Japan. Nevertheless this was the case when the Japanese plate projection system was installed at Woodbridge Park in 1982 and became a vital part of Biddles' up-to-date equipment.

No one of the Biddles family name is active in the firm today. However it has been a family firm in the widest sense: if someone worked for Biddles, they were always keen to get their own relatives into the firm as well. There have been examples of two and three generations working for Biddles spanning 100 years or more of service to a firm whose impact on the world has been a lasting one.

As bookprinters the firm's products are now preserved in copyright libraries and other places, but the printing produced under the heading of 'general and jobbing' is usually ephemeral and intended to be short-lived. The idea of looking after such transient work is fairly new, and compared

with architects and builders, most printers cannot point to many surviving monuments over the years. Yet how valuable for instance, are the 'Guildford Today' surveys which Biddles printed for the local chamber of commerce in the early twentieth century - not only a showcase for local traders but a collection of fascinating early photographs and a description of all town amenities. Thus printing serves the social historian as well as the day-to-day needs of customers.

Now in a new millennium Biddles continues in the tradition of its founders. Biddles continues to embrace the very latest in modern technology using its five high speed Heidleberg Speedmaster presses or its two Timson Web presses - the latest fitted with an ultra violet drier. Digital printing has also been introduced, moving from laser printing, electrophotography, and in May 2000 the company took delivery of the first bookprinting press to use 'magnetography', a printing system which uses the magnetic fields from thousands of micro magnets to create the image to be printed on the system's image cylinder. Meanwhile, in the bindery, the formidable Muller Martini Trendbinder plant allows book binding to take place at a speed which would have been inconceivable only a few short years ago. True the equipment may have changed, but Biddles' philosophy has remained unaltered down the decades - nothing but the best!

Above - all pictures: *Various stages of modern book production.* ***Below:*** *One of Biddles' modern fleet of delivery vehicles.*

The University of Surrey -
a brief history

The Origins of the University go back to a meeting held at Belair Mansion, Dulwich, in the northern part of Surrey in early 1887. Evan Spicer, a city paper merchant and philanthropist, had called together 'a few men of worth' at his home to raise money for Polytechnic Institutes in South London.

Money raising efforts were very successful and, with Evan Spicer as the Chairman of its first Finance Committee, plans were made for a Polytechnic to be built near the Surrey bank of the River Thames. Its foundation stone was laid by the then Prince of Wales on 20th July 1892. The Battersea Polytechnic was officially opened by the Prince and Princess of Wales on 24th February 1894.

In October 1956 the Polytechnic became Battersea College of Technology and it was under that name that it gained its Charter as a the University of Surrey in 1966. Plans for the great moving exercise then began, the Principal of the College, Dr DMA Leggett, became the first Vice Chancellor of the new university. The move was to take four years to complete but eventually

Above: *Belair Mansion, where the origins of the University began.*
Below: *Battersea Park Road, the University's home for almost a century before its move.*

the original building in Battersea Park Road was left behind.

Upon its foundation, one of the most important characteristics of Surrey was that it was a technological university. Whether it was mechanical engineering or music, biology or home economics,

Above: *The University's present premises under construction (top) and from the air.*

each of the courses had some vocational content, some direct aims to the needs of the society into which the student would eventually live and work. An integral feature of most of the courses was that the third year was to be spent in gaining appropriate experience in industry, commerce, local government or social services in this country or overseas. This 'sandwich' principle continues to this day and has proved itself to be of great benefit to the student, to the University and to future employers of the graduates.

There obviously was no actual university on its present site when in 1966 The Lord Robens of Woldingham was inducted as the first Chancellor. The great inaugural ceremony for the new University took place in the Odeon Cinema in

As stated, it took four years for the move to be complete. There was an emergency feeding service on the site situated in a huge marquee. At times the site, on the hillside to the north of the Cathedral, was a sea of mud, completely frozen solid, or 'normal' according to season. The site contained a twelfth century hedge (part of which still remains to this day) and, from the outset, the vision has been to 'look after the environment'. The grounds are extremely well looked after and the world of academia is surrounded by the world of nature. Terry's Pool, at a higher level than the natural pond area was one of the early features of the building programme. ·

Guildford with the Academic Procession moving through the town on its way to the induction. The new Surrey Robes were worn for the first time by all the High Officers.

Top: *The Surrey Robes being worn for the first time for the inaugural ceremony.*
Above left: *Terry's Pool.*

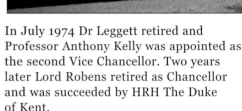

In July 1974 Dr Leggett retired and Professor Anthony Kelly was appointed as the second Vice Chancellor. Two years later Lord Robens retired as Chancellor and was succeeded by HRH The Duke of Kent.

Surrey was the first University in the United Kingdom to award a BA degree in dance.

Situated on the top floor of the University Library the National Resource Centre for Dance, is the only national archive dedicated to dance and movement.

The university buildings containing laboratories, lecture theatres, library, administration offices, restaurants, shops and a students' union building, gradually emerged from the Stag Hill upon which the University and the Cathedral are built.

Student accommodation consists of flats and apartments, the number of which increases annually in an effort to keep pace with the student intake. The original blocks have old Battersea connections (like the Battersea lamp-post that stands between the George Edwards Library and Wates House). Tate, of the sugar family and first Chairman of the Battersea Governors, has been commemorated in this student block.

The Centre holds a vast array of archive materials, and offers a range of services to support education and research in this subject area.

The work of the NRCD falls into several different areas which can broadly be described as: archive collections, publications to support education and research; an annual short course programme for dance teachers; and an information service.

The Centre was established in 1982, following recommendations in the Calouste Gulbenkian Foundation's 1980 report on dance education and training in the UK, and alongside the degree programmes at the University of Surrey. The Centre is a not-for-profit organisation based at the University of Surrey, and the income-generating activities and project funding finance its existence.

Top left: The students' union building.
Top right: One of the students blocks.
Above centre: The logo for the NRCD from the Eileen Pearcey Archive - NRCD.

A Research Park was created in the early 80s to cater for businesses and development agencies to have modern buildings and appropriate environment in which to work. This has grown rapidly through the years and is now an integral part of the economy of the Guildford area.

The Cathedral has become part of the University family. It is used for all degree conferment ceremonies, for University Congregations and some orchestral concerts. This co-operation was cemented by the dedication in 1988 of a special stained glass window in the Cathedral depicting the coats of

arms of the old Battersea Polytechnic and the current University of Surrey.

To mark the Silver Jubilee of the University of Surrey and the Centenary of the Foundation of Battersea Polytechnic, the Queen honoured the University with an official visit in 1991 when she saw something of the variety of work that it undertakes. In April of the same year the Queen's Award for Export Achievement was presented to the University.

In 1994 Dr Kelly retired as Vice Chancellor and was succeeded by Professor Patrick Dowling, the current holder of the post. He took over a very high powered University of Technology that started out monitoring and then building small satellites that

*Top: The Research Park in a picture taken in 1986. **Above left:** The two stained glass windows that depict the old Battersea Polytechnic and the current University of Surrey.*
***Right:** The visit of HRH the Queen in 1991.*

In addition the University provides marvellous facilities for research degrees and the number of research students attaining a second degree increases annually.

The ceremonies in the cathedral are colourful and take us back to medieval England with the colour of the robes and hoods. The ceremony is always presided over by the Chancellor or one of the Pro-Chancellors.

The present University, now often referred to as UniS, continues to build new buildings as its work expands. The latest is one for the European Institute of Health and Medical Sciences which replaces the old Robens Institute. This huge building sends a message out to the people of Guildford, proclaiming technology for the twenty-first century.

has now reached the status of having Surrey Space Centre and Surrey Satellite Technology Ltd within its grounds. Some of the items circling above us on a daily basis started their life on Stag Hill.

EH Shepard, the illustrator of Winnie the Pooh, Punch, and many other books lived for the majority of his life in Guildford. In 1972, four years before his death, he personally presented to the University the residue of his illustrations, manuscripts, notes, etc. This gift is now the EH Shepard Archive which is probably the most authoritative archive of Shepard's work containing over fourteen hundred of his drawings as well as his papers.

The main purpose of any University is that of education, not just education in a given subject but education for life. The old word 'college' meant a place where people lived together and although in the twenty-first century this means there are a few thousand people living together on the campus at Guildford, they all must benefit from rubbing shoulders with each other. The ultimate aim, however, (at least to the parents of the students) is graduation as the fulfilment of four years of study.

Top left: *Professor Martin Sweeting.*
Top right: *One of EH Shephard's sketches.*
Right: *One of the colourful ceremonies held at the cathedral.*

Shopping in the footsteps of our ancestors

The Friary Centre was built in 1980 and is now jointly owned by Westfield and MEPC. It rose on the eyesore of land that was home to derelict warehouses and remnants of the old Friary Brewery. MEPC turned four acres of red brick and rubble into a modern precinct and shopping centre. It brought to Guildford the convenience of traffic free shopping, an airy and light atmosphere to make the life of the consumer that little bit easier. Trading began in November 1980, though the official opening ceremony took place the following June. Princess Alexandra performed the honours. Major refurbishment by MEPC began in 1988. Facilities were updated and more natural light introduced into the complex. The first phase was completed in September when 21 new retail outlets were created. The second phase, completed the following year in October 1989, advanced the centre's design. Glass sided lifts and shiny new escalators, topped off by the new skylit glass atrium and the breathtaking new North Street entrance, gave the Friary a futuristic look. The Roof Garden Food Court and the ground floor Le Boulevard cafe were created. The former, which opened in June 1990, soon became the focal point for shoppers relaxing in its garden style environment. This refurbishment programme cost in the region of £20 million and resulted in 30,000 sq feet of extra retail space as well as an improved shopping experience.

MEPC has developed a reputation for being a company that wants more from its projects than just a healthy turnover. Its commitment to improving the lives and environment of those who shop within its properties is a matter of record.

*Above: An artists impression of Phase One of the Friary Shopping Centre. **Below:** The Friary Meux brewery before its demise in the 1970s.*

Dishonour' with good reason.

In the early years of the 17th century the land came into the possession of John Murray. It cost him just a few hundred pounds. Imagine the price that such valuable building land would command in the 21st century! Murray, a confidante of the king, was created a peer in 1622, becoming Viscount Annandale. In 1630

The original Friary was founded in 1274 by Queen Eleanor of Provence. She was the wife of Henry III. Their grandson, Henry, died as a young child. The Friary was established by the Dominicans as an epitaph to the young prince who had drawn his last breath in Guildford and whose heart is said to have been preserved in the Friary Chapel. Roughly 20 monks lived here on average during the 14th and 15th centuries. However, by the time of Henry VIII the number had dwindled to just seven. The king embarked on his policy of dissolution of the monasteries and Guildford's links with the noble friars were severed. The Friary and all its contents were turned over to the Crown. The church that had stood on the site was demolished and some of its materials used to build Henry VIII's 'House of Honour' that was erected in the grounds for him to enjoy. His enemies called it the 'House of

he began building a fine mansion of chalk and flint, but did not live long enough to enjoy it. He passed away in 1640. Charles II is said to have been a royal visitor in later years when he is reputed to have stayed at the mansion in 1671.

By the middle of the 18th century the house had passed into the hands of the Onslow family. The river wharf close by was a dangerous place. Although it was profitable to charge tolls on the tonnage the barges carried, there was always a chance of being blown to smithereens by the collection of gunpowder mills that operated in the near vicinity.

Top: *Archaealogical excavations under way prior to building the shopping centre.* ***Above left:*** *The Friary Shopping centre shortly after opening.*

In 1794 the house was taken back into state ownership, this time by the government rather than the Crown. The house was converted into barracks and offices, but was finally laid to rest in 1818 when it was demolished. Part of the site became a cricket ground before being laid out as Friary Place in the 1840s. The remainder of the site was leased to a brewer. Friary Meux Brewery became a familiar landmark in more recent times. As with so many independent brewers it was eventually swallowed up by one of the big boys. Allied Breweries was the beneficiary. Brewing ceased in 1969 and MEPC took over the site in 1972.

Before commencing its building of the shopping centre the company had to give consideration to what lay beneath the ground it was to excavate. Down beneath the soil were many relics of the priors and friars who had prayed and worked there seven centuries ago. Carefully picking their way through the voids

Right: *The Friary Shopping centre following refurbishment.* **Below:** *An aerial view of Guildford showing the Shopping Centre near the top of the picture.*

underneath the old chapter house and cloisters some graves and tombs were uncovered. In 1978 more extensive archaeological work was done before the major excavations for the new shopping centre were started in earnest. Some artefacts were found, including rings, brooches and clasps. Although some of the graves had been subjected to the attention of grave robbers in previous centuries quite a few survived to tell the historical tale. Despite the absence of many complete skeletons there was still enough evidence to suggest that bodies were laid out in one of three positions. Hands were crossed over the chest, over the pelvis or laid by the side. Five skeletons were discovered in a single grave with their arms linked, suggesting

they perished during an epidemic or plague. There were skeletons of young infants discovered, but few of childen older than five.

That seemed to imply that those who survived their first few years in this world generally went on to reach adulthood. All this information and the various odds and ends of jewellery and pottery were passed on to Guildford Museum. MEPC played its part in preserving the heritage of the town and illustrated in practical terms what its mission statement and company policy professed on paper.

In 2000 new plans were unveiled by MEPC for a further major retail development scheme. The St Dominic development was to be built adjacent to the Friary Shopping Centre. It was to have the involvement of an important department store and include 45 new retail units. Included in the package was the regeneration of the bus station and improvements to the look of North Street. The old Barclays Bank building was earmarked for linked residential conversion. Just as the Friary Centre was built on an untidy and unsightly area of the town in 1980, so this project was to give new life to over five acres of partially derelict land. Guildford has been losing the pre-eminence it once held as an attractive place to come and shop. MEPC's plans are that the town centre is restored as an attractive and modern shopping area, whilst retaining its sense of history and tradition. Two years previously the company had received planning permission to develop the retail

and residential amenities. Further examination showed that too much was expected of the site and the latest blueprint was judged to provide a more realistic outcome.

The new St Dominic Centre provides additional employment opportunities for the region as it will take some 850 staff to run the shops. The centre also provides opportunities to leave the car at home for a change with its excellent links to public transport, provision for cyclists and encouragement to pedestrians. The Friary and St Dominic Centres are the way forward, but they have managed to integrate the traditions and history of their locality.

Above: *An interior view of the shopping centre in the early 1980s.* ***Below:*** *The impressive new main entrance to The Friary, dated 1990.*

Transforming Guildford

For most of us electricity is mystery. Why doesn't it leak out when one removes a light bulb from its socket? What is the difference between ohms and volts, and where does electricity go to after it has been used? Until a couple of centuries ago such questions were unheard of; not until the experiments of Galvani who showed that an electrical spark would make a dead frog's leg twitch (and so inspire Mary Shelley to write Frankenstein) did the world wake up to the existence of electricity. And not until the work of Michael Faraday, that self educated genius who created the first electric motor, did anyone think that electricity might have any practical use other than giving the public electric shocks in various enterprises involving medical quackery.

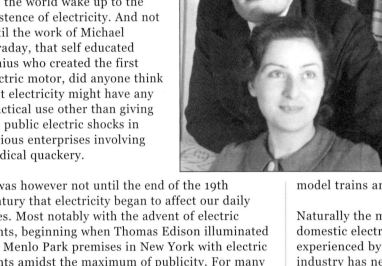

It was however not until the end of the 19th century that electricity began to affect our daily lives. Most notably with the advent of electric lights, beginning when Thomas Edison illuminated his Menlo Park premises in New York with electric lights amidst the maximum of publicity. For many in Britain their first taste of electric illumination came with Buffalo Bill Cody and his Wild west Show which was one of the first such touring shows to carry its own portable generators.

Interestingly one of the original methods of distribution to homes were the power lines installed for tramways, power being drawn down from the overhead wires and the tram companies becoming electricity suppliers as well as tramway operators.

Electricity, its production and use, have grown ever more complicated during the passing years. One real problem was in lowering a mains voltage down to a level appropriate to the appliance it would be used with. In Britain we use 240 volts in our homes, a voltage which has been reduced by electrical transformers from the thousands of volts being transmitted along power lines from the power stations. And once in our home the voltage is often reduced still further to power small appliances which need even less than 240 volts such as alarm clocks, model trains and telephones.

Naturally the minor concerns of the supply of domestic electricity are trivial compared to those experienced by industry. Equipment used in industry has need of not only transformers to

Above: *Frederick Cowley pictured with his first wife Doris.* ***Below:*** *A view of one of the bays at Transformers & Rectifiers Ltd, Woodbridge Meadows.*

reduce or increase voltage but also uses delicate equipment which may need a non-fluctuating supply of electricity to ensure precise levels of power. Similarly in order to ensure that electrical equipment including transformers, rectifiers and generators are working exactly as they should, quality testing equipment is needed. The market for such equipment is complemented by Guildford's own T&R Group.

The T&R Group was founded in August 1951 by Frederick Thomas Cowley. 'T&R' simply standing for Transformers and Rectifiers. Previously Frederick had been the chief engineer for a Croydon-based company which manufactured transformers and rectifiers. Unhappy with the company's managing director Frederick Cowley decided to go it alone.

Setting up in Guildford and helped by his wife Sophia 'Doris' Cowley, Frederick's fledgling firm occupied its original premises, an old barn in Honeypot Lane (behind where the Yvonne Arnaud theatre now is) for ten years until 1961. The business used winding machines for winding electrical coils and guillotines for copper and electrical steel sheet. Today similar machines are used though now everything is bigger, better and needless to say there are many more of them.

That first year sales amounted to just £2,000. Frederick got the orders and did the designs and drawings whilst Doris took care of the office work. The firm began to employ staff almost immediately

Top: An aerial view of the Groups Head Office at Woodbridge Meadows. Right: Frederick and Anne Cowley during a cruise on board the QE2 in 1994.

and grew considerably over the course of the next ten years.

In fact the business grew at a remarkable pace over those few short years; it moved and expanded into the present factory in Woodbridge Meadows in 1961 after the council approached the firm offering it a 99 year lease if it built its own factory. The new premises had just two storeys to begin with - a third was added later and subsequently another bay. By the time the firm moved to Woodbridge Meadows the company was employing up to forty people and now the Group employs approximately 200.

The first of many strategic acquisitions was made in 1968 when Transformers & Rectifiers Ltd bought out Partridge Transformers Ltd.

Most of the work was for industry rather than for the government or public utilities. By the 1970s the firm faced fierce competition from other companies but those challenges were short-lived given the efficiency of the firm and its solid financial position, not least the advantage of owning its own premises.

Transformers & Rectifiers Ltd went on to become the foremost privately owned manufacturer in the United Kingdom helped by demand from overseas to supply furnace transformers.

Today most of the Group's sales go abroad, the majority going to the middle east and far east.

Problems getting established in the US markets led, in 1982, to the setting up of T&R Holdings Ltd. By 1983 the T&R Group of companies comprised of the original T&R company - or more correctly Transformers and Rectifiers Ltd - set up in 1951, T&R Generators Ltd incorporated in 1975, T&R Welding Products Ld which came into existence in 1978 and T&R Test Equipment Ltd established in 1981.

Subsequently the group has expanded by further acquisitions the first being the firm of Burnett International Ltd, which was bought in 1983, a generator exporter which Frederick Cowley bought up in order to boost the sales of T&R Generators Ltd.

Today the Group employs 200 staff and is the only company in the country manufacturing transformers, rectifiers and regulators under one roof.

Sadly Doris Cowley died in 1990 following some years of ill health. Frederick Cowley continued with the business, a year later acquiring Southern Transformer Products in Twickenham which had itself earlier acquired the business interests of

Top: T&R Generators first premises at Bramley. ***Above centre:*** *An interior view of one of the bays at Keens Lane factory in the 1980s.* ***Above:*** *An aerial view of Keens Lane premises which houses T&R Generators Ltd, T&R Test Equipment Ltd and Burnett International Ltd.*

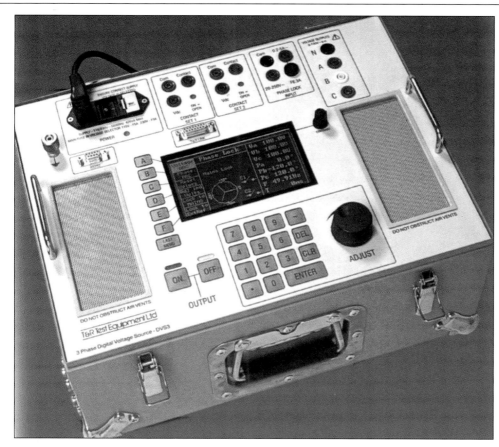

internationally for its expertise in the design, engineering and manufacture of electrical equipment and plant. The Group's product range includes electrical transformers and regulators, power rectifiers, specialist welding alloys and consumables, engine driven generating sets, high voltage and heavy current test equipment.

The group now operates from three factory complexes in and around Guildford and offers a complete service in terms of design and manufacture.

Gresham Transformers Ltd. In the process of investigating Southern Transformers Frederick Cowley would meet the woman who would become his second wife, Anne, who was Company Secretary and accountant there.

The owner of Southern Transformer Products had approached Frederick Cowley to see if he might be interested in buying it since the business was in difficulties. Frederick visited the company and bought it within a couple of weeks of seeing it; during his visit he asked Anne, the Company Secretary, to come to Guildford for a meeting - where she stayed to work for him.

Most recently the T&R group bought Brentford Electric Ltd, part of the Allenwest group, which made regulators transformers and rectifiers at Crawley. Southern Transformers and the Brentford company have now been brought together under the T&R name.

Frederick and Anne Cowley married in 1999; it was definitely a red letter year when Frederick was also awarded an MBE in the New Year Honours List for services to the electrical engineering industry, receiving his award at Buckingham Palace.

Still active in the business which he founded five decades ago Frederick Cowley today lives in Farley Green, Guildford, Surrey with is wife Anne. Frederick Cowley's T&R Group is known

Top: A digital testing unit. **Right:** *Frederick and Anne Cowley at Buckingham Palace where Frederick received the MBE.*

At the start of the third millennium electricity is everywhere; in our homes, cars and places of work. It is hard to believe that within living memory gas lighting was still common, that computers were unheard of and that in the homes which did have electricity use it was often limited to a few light sockets and an electric iron.

In industry the use of electricity is universal. Machines driven by belting taking power from a steam engine have disappeared to be replaced by machines dependant upon a suitable supply of electricity. There is no end in sight to further development nor any foreseeable slackening of demand. The T&R group clearly has a future as dynamic as its past.

Quality and innovation - an enduring partnership

When Lewis & Hickey opened an office in Guildford in 1963 it was already a well established firm which had been practising in London since 1894. It had been founded in the City of London as W A Lewis. Pat Hickey and Norman Lewis became partners in the business in 1930 but it wasn't until 1946 that the practice was known as Lewis & Hickey. In fact the move out of London and the establishment of the Guildford office came at an exciting time for the company as the following year five new partners including Liam Martin, the company's present Senior Partner, were appointed.

The practice offers a wide range of services, a result of an ongoing desire to provide clients with the expertise they require to build attractive and workable buildings but it is the long association with Marks & Spencer which has provided a basis for the firm's reputation and expansion. It sometimes happens that seemingly chance events provide the catalyst for others which have a major impact on society, and the fact that the Lewis architects had been responsible for the design of a new multi storey office building called Friendly House at 21-23 Chiswell Street in the City of London was the means by which the practice came into contact with Marks & Spencer, which was moving away from its market stall origins and was seeking permanent shop premises (it had long abandoned its 'don't ask the price, it's a penny' philosophy). The original client needed only the upper floors for its offices and so the ground floor and basement of this building was leased to M & S as its new London Head Office. M & S's agreement to the practice's design for a shop front is recorded in the office diary for February 1921. A covenant required the Company to provide separate toilet facilities for the part of the building it occupied; the Lewis practice was commissioned to provide these and company records for December 1922 show an acceptance of a quotation of £125 for the work. Eventually additional building work was undertaken and the final cost was £200, for which the practice fee was £10.

Above: Mr Liam Martin, current senior partner who has been with the paractice since 1959.
Below: Architect's drawing for the Marks & Spencer store at Orchard House, Marble Arch.

Thus, in 1924 Marks & Spencer occupied its first London Head Office and there began also Lewis & Hickey's unique association with the company which has continued unbroken to this day, covering the design of several further Head Office, Social, Computer, Warehouse and Store Buildings involving many thousands of commissions in the intervening period. In 1926 M & S was interested in accelerating its expansion programme and to achieve this, four teams of independent Consultants comprising Architects, Structural Engineers and Quantity Surveyors were appointed on a geographical basis. Lewis & Hickey, already established as a consultant to the company, was to act in one of the teams and to operate mainly in the southern half of England and Wales.

At that time there were 135 stores, but an unprecedented era in building began resulting in 99 new stores and numerous extensions up to 1939. But more significantly foundations had also been laid for a new philosophy of retailing and building which was to set the trend in both industries for the fifty years that followed and beyond. This philosophy and the association of the two companies have made an unrivalled contribution to the architectural and social fabric of our towns and cities, in a combined and persistent quest for excellence in the erection of these buildings in the years 1923 to the present day.

Above, both pictures: Just two of the Marks and Spencer Lutyens influenced facades designed by Lewis & Hickey. Right: Patrick Hickey who was senior partner for almost 40 years.

Research as always preceded design and building, and continued throughout, resulting in high quality, speedy erection and an individual personality which was to become a hall-mark of the company's buildings. The original elevation of the Winchester store was completed in 1924, the Georgian style and the use of brick and stone achieved harmony within the town, and this was regarded as one of the most beautiful store buildings of the period.

The programme of expansion and development, initiated in the previous decade, gained momentum in the 1930s. Interest in research increased covering such areas as choice of sites, building materials, speed of building and building costs. Many of the ideas born then are still relevant today. Stores were generally constructed using steel frames and timber joisted floors and flat roofs, with finishes chosen for their qualities of hygiene, durability, appearance and simplicity of erection. Elevations were individually designed to suit the scale of their surroundings and to express the dignity and importance of their purpose. The stores, at Brixton, Canterbury, Islington, Putney, Woolwich and The Pantheon Oxford Street, had set a new standard in the use of both building materials and methods. The company's philosophy of care for its staff extended to its building sites and set standards which were later enacted in legislation.

It was during this period in 1935 that the practice

Head Office in Baker Street was acquired and equipped to meet the needs of an expanding organisation. Food and Textile laboratories were installed and the new automatic telephone exchange was stated at the time to be equivalent to that required for a small town.

completed a new store in Guildford for Marks and Spencer in the building occupied since 1962 by Boots the Chemist and who is today one of Lewis & Hickey's most prolific clients.

The outbreak of war ended development and expansion although interest in research continued. New methods of construction resulted from mechanisation and the increased use of plastics and metal alloys. The re-planning of war devastated city centres presented new opportunities in the 1950s. Marks & Spencer re-formed the Development Team and was eager to put its war-time research into practice. Rehabilitation of damaged stores was a first consideration. New sites were made available by local authorities and new stores often offered twice or three times the previous retail space. These new stores were of fire-resisting construction with new fire and safety installations and up-to-date staff amenities. With larger stores, engineering services became an increasing element in the content and costs of new developments. In 1955 the present

The 1960s was a time of major extensions and rebuilding programmes; two new larger stores were built to replace the existing stores at Guildford and Tooting. The Guildford store was constructed on the site of 'Whites' Department Store to replace the existing smaller store in Surrey's County Town. This store was originally designed to allow for two further storeys, a sign of the optimism of the time. These have subsequently been constructed during the several developments which have taken place since its original completion. In 1966 the basement was converted to a salesfloor and a first floor stock room

Top, both pictures: A striking design for both the interior and exterior of Bhs. Right: Guildford's Marks and Spencer store completed in 1962. Far right: A Burger King interior.

of its staff and comfort of its customers continued to have implications for building design; stores now needed specially equipped toilets, ramps and automatic doors, and air conditioning of salesfloors had become the established standard practice; this soon became a requirement for office and staff quarters as a further amenity for M & S personnel.

Lewis & Hickey continues to respond to developments in the retail scene. A feature of the last twenty years or so has been its expanding retail service to clients such as Boots, Borders, Bhs, Debenhams, Gap, Heatons in Ireland, Mango in Budapest, Warsaw and Prague and others. Office developments in the UK, Prague and Ireland as well as commissions from Barclays, The Royal Bank of Scotland, McDonalds and residential developments are now extensively undertaken.

The 1990s witnessed a great extension of services offered by the company, including the addition of interior design, town planning, project and safety management, shopfit, engineering services and research and development. Practice offices are today successfully operating in Guildford, London, Edinburgh and Nottingham in the UK and also in Dublin and Prague in Europe. Lewis & Hickey offer an extensive range of expertise in architectural services and is poised to continue the practice's achievements of appropriate and quality design in the century ahead and is soon to commence an extensive development of its Guildford office premises at 18 Farnham Road.

constructed which was later converted to a salesfloor in 1973. In 1979 a second floor stockroom was added and the basement salesfloor enlarged. In 1983 a ramped access from North Street and automatic doors were added, providing a much appreciated facility for the handicapped and aged. On the dining room wall hangs a specially commissioned oil painting by the artist to Lewis & Hickey, the late Stuart Milner RWS, RBA, of a seventeenth century scene in Guildford High Street. It was presented to the store by the practice at the time of the original opening in 1962.

The 1970s were years of consolidation and development and the practice was responsible for numerous new warehouses, including that at White City. The renowned M & S concern for the welfare

Top left: *Surrey Research Park.* **Top right:** *An interior's for WH Smith, Guildford.* **Above left:** *New office headquarters in Prague in 1998 for Volkswagon/Skoda.* **Right:** *Michael Gallagher, Managing Partner, joined the practice in 1966.*

Location, location, location!

What cost £18,600 in 1972 and £535,000 in 1999? The answer is a farmhouse in Bramley, sold twice, 27 years apart, by Guildford estate agents, surveyors and auctioneers, Clarke Gammon. How property prices have changed!

Clarke Gammon is one of the longest established businesses in Guildford High Street. Many thousands of Guildford residents will have used the firm's services over the decades when buying or selling their homes, renting premises or buying and selling antiques and fine art at the firm's sale rooms. The firm was founded in 1919 by Sidney Clarke and Frank Gammon, both of whom had recently returned to their native Guildford after serving in France during the Great War. At first the firm was based in offices in the Upper High Street.

Sidney Clarke was an auctioneer and estate agent, Frank Gammon was a surveyor; together they combined their talents and established a firm in which providing a complete professional and personal service became the hallmark of the business.

In 1927 Clarke Gammon bought the old established business of Emerys from its then proprietor, A Portsmouth. For many years thereafter the firm would be known as Clarke, Gammon & Emerys. W Emery had opened a tobacconist's shop at 70 High Street in 1873 and, in 1880, diversified becoming a curious hybrid, a tobacconist/auctioneer; that business moved to 71 (now 45) High Street in around 1890. Those premises are still Clarke Gammon's main offices today.

Around the same time as it bought 45 High Street the partnership also acquired auction rooms off North Street, which subsequently relocated to Walnut Tree Close and then Bedford Road where the present sale rooms are to be found.

Sidney Clarke's son Brian Clarke and brother-in-law Colin Trent joined the partnership after the second world war. Later Colin's son Michael Trent, and Roger Lawson, joined the partnership.

Above: *The original Clarke Gammon premises at 188 High Street, now demolished.* ***Below:*** *A corner of the furniture auction rooms at 26 High Street.*

valued firm. With offices in London's Mayfair as well as in High Street, Godalming and Middle Street Shere, and the Guildford residential team now in Quarry Street, the firm is able to offer wide marketing which includes not only London purchasers but also overseas buyers.

Additionally the firm also offers a comprehensive service regarding a wide range of shops, office and industrial premises, advice on such issues as landlord and tenant lease renewals, rent reviews, rating, leasehold reform, property taxation and insurance. Clarke Gammon's long experience in the lettings market enables it to provide expert advice to landlords regarding every aspect of property lettings together with a wide range of services, from simply finding a tenant to ongoing rent collection and full property management. The firm also acts as Managing Agents for the Residents Associations of apartment blocks.

The partnership chose to remain independent of the large groups into which many other established estate agents have merged, in order to maintain professional independence and impartiality, and to be free from the distracting involvement of selling financial and ancillary services.

The values established by Sidney Clarke and Frank Gammon remain at the core of the service provided by the firm which they founded and Clarke Gammon remains dedicated to providing a complete, personal and professional service to clients.

Today, the partnership comprises Michael Trent who manages the Professional and Commercial Department, Peter Hunt who runs the Survey and Management Department whilst, in addition, a new third partner, Tony Jamieson, heads the Residential Department.

Regular auction sales, run by Brian Clarke's son Stephen Clarke with the Manager, Gordon Patrick, are held at the firm's sale rooms which enjoy a unique reputation and atmosphere built up over many years. As fine art auctioneers and valuers the firm takes pride in offering a complete service to clients advising both on the sale and acquisition of fine antiques and chattels. Free valuations to potential auction clients are given at the sale rooms or, in the case of larger items, at the homes of clients.

As for the sale of residential property, Clarke Gammon provides a professional service which combines quality marketing with enthusiasm, efficiency and commitment. And if 'location, location, location' are the estate agents traditional response to the question 'what three factors most influence property prices' then Clarke Gammon's own location makes it a highly

*Above left: A rear view before the construction of Phoenix Court. **Top left:** Clarke Gammon & Emerys' office on the High Street in 1960.*
***Below:** A collection of Doulton china which passed through the sale room in 1999.*

The company famed for its warmth

What do Sir Paul McCartney, Sir Elton John and Freddie Mercury all have in common? One answer is that they have all been clients of the renowned Guildford heating company DH Bryant Ltd.

The company founder, Denis Bryant, served an apprenticeship as a plumber with the well-known building firm, Tribe & Robinson. Denis learnt all the old trade skills including working with lead. During that period he worked on the lead on the Guildford Guildhall clock when it was refixed above the High Street after the end of the second world war.

Denis started working for himself in 1951 living with his family above his parents' grocery shop, W Bryant, at 6 Station Road. At that time his mother would take telephone calls for grocery deliveries intermingled with reports of burst pipes.

Having served an apprenticeship where he had to travel to sites by bicycle, not only carrying his tools but sometimes a wash basin as well, Denis had realised the importance of transport; he sold his motor bike to buy a second hand van for £100.

Denis married Sheila Brande in 1953 and they moved to 46 Station Road to live with Sheila's parents and where Denis had his first real office. Naturally Sheila did much of the administration work and answered the telephone.

Initially materials were stored in the basement but more space was

needed. For a period a coach garage at the stables behind Findon Lodge, Christmas Hill, Shalford was used to store plumbing materials and as a workshop.

Before long several men were being employed It was at that time, 1955, that Bob Payne joined the firm as an apprentice: having worked through every aspect of the business he would eventually become its managing director.

In the early days of heating the main fuel had been solid fuel but oil had increased in favour to the extent that within a few days of the Suez Crisis arising in 1956 the whole company order book was cancelled. The firm had to rapidly return to the plumbing field and developing the gas heating market. The strong team spirit of the staff ensured survival by being prepared to tackle any job.

In 1957 the Bryants moved to their current premises, 33 Station Road, previously a builder's house, store and yard. Initially the office was a room in the house, and a very small outbuilding.

In those days all the traditional materials were used: steel, cast iron, copper pipe work, cast iron radiators, copper sheeting and lead. The skills used included cutting, threading, hydraulic bending and forge bending of large steel pipes, the use of molten lead to make joints in cast iron pipes, molten lead to make toy soldiers, forming lead or copper roofing, lead burning, wiping joints on lead pipes, soldering and brazing copper pipes and welding steel.

Top left: *Denis Bryant.*
Above: *The plaque from Denis's first vehicle.* **Far right:** *The first company van.* **Right:** *Denis's wife, Sheila.*

In 1970 Bob Payne established the relationship with a London based, high class builder/ decorator which moved the company into its unique position in the luxury home market. Although the majority of projects are based in London, it has been the cornerstone of the business ever since, enabling the company to withstand the crippling construction industry recession in the 1990s.

Over the years the company has attracted and trained a loyal group of skilled, professional engineers and staff. Many started straight from school and now have up to 40 years invaluable experience.

After the death of its founder in 1988 the company has continued under the direction of Bob Payne and Gordon Bryant. Now the majority of the workload is large heating and water service installations with a smaller proportion of plumbing and air conditioning. The company has become well known for its high quality design and installation standards and has clocked up an extraordinary client list including not only pop megastars but also an unusual number of other well known institutions and celebrities. The business has come a long way since Denis Bryant first got on his motor bike.

As the firm increased in size so did its administration; it also became orientated towards heating - so facilities were needed for design, estimating and most essentially, a boiler maintenance department.

In 1959/60 an office was built behind the house to accommodate an accounts office and a design/estimating department. Gordon Bryant joined the company in 1961 as a student apprentice to be trained at the National College of Heating, Ventilation and Air Conditioning. That training gave the company the expertise, confidence and the design capability to branch out into larger contract work including commercial and industrial buildings. Within only a few years, the company's work range expanded from heating of normal housing with 15 to 70 KW boilers to the heating of multi-storey offices, factories, training centres for the disabled with boiler plant up to 1500 KW. The wide customer base is still maintained by the company.

The firm became a limited company in 1960. In 1964/65 they applied for planning permission to convert the house to offices. Aerial photographs illustrated the extent of commercial properties in the road.

Top: The shop at 6 Station Road. ***Above left:*** *An aerial view of Shalford, with the extent of the firm's premises highlighted.* ***Above right:*** *One of the firm's fleet of vans.* ***Below left:*** *Bob Payne.* ***Below right:*** *Gordon Bryant.*

Christianity in Healthcare
Mount Alvernia Hospital

The inspiration for a thriving modern Guildford hospital was the life of Saint Francis of Assisi. Francis was a radical reformer who lived in the 13th century. His passionate commitment to Christ led him to a life of utter poverty in the service of the poor. At the end of his life he told those who sought to copy his example, 'I have done what was mine to do, may Christ teach you what you are to do'. Countless men and women in each succeeding century have been challenged by his words as they sought to do for Christ what was uniquely theirs to do.

Three women formed a Catholic Franciscan community at Holly Place, London, caring for orphan children and bringing the same tender concern to the poor of the area, as Francis had done in his native Assisi.

This community grew and was eventually to result in a community of sisters opening an orphanage in Aldershot in 1902. The sisters'

Right: A view of Hill House, from the rear, in 1936. Glaven can be seen to the right hand side. *Below: Glaven seen from the rear. The link between the two houses can be seen in the centre of the picture.*

special interest in health care dates from 1925, when it became evident that, for the healthy development of the children in their care, some of the sisters needed to be nurses. Two sisters, Francis Spring and Teresa Grant, were therefore sent to train as nurses in St John's and St Elizabeth's Hospital in London. Once Sister Francis had completed her training she went to work in Aldershot hospital and it was here that she met the surgeon Mr Gerald Steele. His encouragement strengthened Sister Francis' dream of opening a nursing home staffed by sisters and eventually, in 1935 the Congregation took a new step in its history by opening Mount Alvernia Hospital in Guildford. This occupied two Victorian houses, Hill House which had

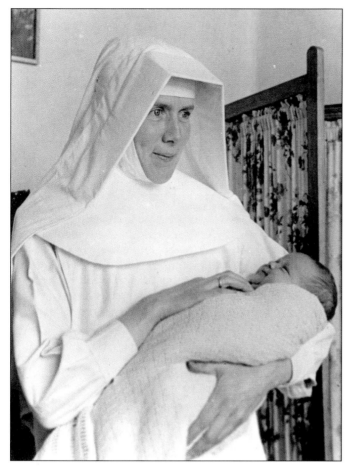

attentive to the physical, psychological and spiritual aspects of the lives of their patients and seek to help them attain healing, wholeness, harmony and inner peace.

In keeping with the long Christian tradition of offering hospitality, Mount Alvernia considers it very important to provide a warm, welcoming and peaceful atmosphere which is conducive to holistic healing.

served as a temporary war hospital in 1918 and Glaven which had been an Anglican rectory; these houses were linked together to form a 17 bed low cost nursing and maternity home in the days before the existence of the National Health Service.

The name Mount Alvernia was chosen to link it with Mount La Verna, in Tuscany near Assisi where St Francis loved to pray and prepare for his ministry.

From its humble beginnings, Mount Alvernia began to grow. Many young women became Sisters and were trained in a variety of healthcare and other professions. This enabled the Congregation to send many sisters as missionaries around the world, spreading the Christian approach to health care far and wide. During the second world war, the hospital played its part as an emergency hospital. This included caring for many London evacuees and their new-born babies.

All health care offered at Mount Alvernia is based on the belief that men and women are made in the likeness of God and are therefore entitled to respect. The belief that people are not just bodies to care for, but a complex interplay of mind, body and spirit is also a fundamental concept. As a result the staff are

As the hospital is run out of a desire to show God's healing love for all people, only the highest standards are considered appropriate and all members of staff strive for excellence in everything they undertake. The professional and personal development of the staff is encouraged and supported. For the same reason the Christian principles of integrity and justice are upheld which affects relationships with patients, their relatives and all with whom they do business.

Mount Alvernia underwent major refurbishment between 1990 and 1999 and is now a spacious, well-planned hospital with 76 beds, furnished and equipped to a high standard. The hospital offers a full range of medical care and is accredited by an external Hospital Accreditation Quality Programme (HAP).

Above left: Sister Margaret Keenan with one of the 20,000 babies that were born in the Maternity unit prior to it's closure in 1989. Above right: The front door of the hospital in 1940. Right: The modern Mount Alvernia Hospital.

The firm from Godalming that's a powerful force across the world

An international business with wide-ranging capabilities across several disciplines in the fields of engineering and construction, which began as a consulting practice in Westminster in 1889, is now based in Godalming. The same site is also home to the original water wheel which in 1881 supplied the power for the world's first public electricity supply system.

Although vastly different in terms of scale and scope of operations from the original endeavour, the company has grown, mainly by adhering to and carrying forward the principles of technical excellence and encouraging the sheer genius of innovative engineering, which was the characteristic of the founder, Alexander Kennedy.

Kennedy had been appointed Professor of Engineering by University College London at the remarkably young age of twenty-eight; the research experience he built up during his fourteen years in the post proved invaluable to him in his consulting engineer's practice. His earliest assignments were power generation and distribution projects for the Westminster Electric Supply Corporation in London and Glasgow. Bernard Jenkin became a partner in 1899 and the scope of Kennedy & Jenkin widened to include railway electrification and tramways.

In 1905 Alexander was knighted. He became President of the Institution of Civil Engineers in 1906 and he took his son, John, as well as Sydney Donkin into partnership in 1908. In 1914 Kennedy & Donkin was formed, establishing a name that was to become synonymous with quality and reliability of service through to the new millennium.

During this period the firm was heavily involved in the establishment of the national power supply grid in the UK. John Kennedy received his knighthood in 1943.

After the second world war, the firm expanded its work outside the UK, particularly to Africa and

Above left: *Sir Alexander B W Kennedy FRS.* ***Right:*** *A portrait of S B Donkin from 1943.* ***Below:*** *The interior of Battersea Power Station in 1901.*

Partnership and Applied Geology), changing its name to Rust Kennedy & Donkin.

Major contracts for the supply of architectural design services to Cheshire County Council and the provision of management and maintenance of the Highways Agency Area 5 also brought added expertise in building and facilities management and motorway and highway maintenance.

The late 1990s were a period of reorganisation culminating in the purchase of the company by leading New York based international engineering and programme management consultancy, Parsons Brinckerhoff.

Parsons Brinckerhoff can also trace its history back to 1885 when William Barclay Parsons established himself as a consulting engineer at 22 William Street in New York. He was later joined by Henry Brinckerhoff and from an initial involvement in the construction of the New York City Subway in 1890, the practice has over the years been associated with many major infrastructure projects, including the Fort McHenry Tunnel - an 8,000 foot eight lane structure under Baltimore Harbour, which in 1985 was the largest underwater tunnel in the world.

In 1995 PB had acquired Merz and McLellan, another century-old engineering consultancy based in Newcastle, and in November 1999 the energy divisions of Kennedy & Donkin and Merz and McLellan joined forces to become PB Power - the largest power consultancy in the UK .

Having traded as Kennedy & Donkin for almost 90 years, a decision was made at the end of the year 2000 to build on the reputation and recognition of the parent company by adopting the name Parsons Brinckerhoff across the company's operations in Europe, Africa and the Middle East.

Top: *The original water wheel at Westbrook Mills.* ***Above left:*** *Her Majesty the Queen Mother officially opening Hunterston Power Station.* ***Below:*** *An aerial view of Parsons Brinckerhoff's offices in Godalming.*

the Middle East, working on new hydroelectric schemes at Aswan (Egypt) and the Mass Rapid Transit System in Hong Kong.

In the early 1980s the 4 acre site at Westbrook Mills was acquired. By 1983 new purpose-built headquarters for the firm had been designed and constructed, accommodating in excess of 300 technical, professional and support staff.

A merger with Henderson Busby International in 1986 brought into the firm expertise in railway, highway and bridge engineering. Henderson Busby could trace its roots back to 1862.

In addition to a long involvement with the design of trains, maintenance vehicles and safety aspects of the Channel Tunnel, the firm has also had a ten-year association with the Docklands Light Railway and has provided consultancy design services for the light rail schemes at Croydon, Manchester, Sheffield and the West Midlands.

In 1987 the firm restructured from a partnership into a group of limited companies privately owned by its senior engineers. The Duke of Gloucester was the principal guest at the celebrations to mark the firm's centenary on 9 June 1989.

In 1994 the company was sold to WMX Technologies Inc. in the USA, and at the same time joined other international consulting companies in the Rust consulting group (including MRM

The increase in traffic on High Street was a problem even in 1938 as can be seen in this photograph

Acknowledgments

Peter Sherwood
Clare Miles of Surrey University's Guildford Institute
Matthew Alexander and his colleagues at Guildford Museum
Geoff Mayhew and Jo Holland of Cornhill Insurance plc
Trevor Fisher and Graham Collyer of the Surrey Advertiser

Thanks are also due to
Andrew Mitchell who penned the editorial text and
Judith Dennis for her copywriting skills